YOUTH AND THE LAW

YOUTH AND THE LAW

UNDERSTANDING CANADIAN LAW

DANIEL J. BAUM

DUNDURN
TORONTO

Editors: Katie Scott and Michael Melgaard
Design: Jesse Hooper
Printer: Webcom

Library and Archives Canada Cataloguing in Publication

Baum, Daniel Jay, 1934-, author
    Youth and the law / Daniel J. Baum.

(Understanding Canadian law ; number 1)
Includes index.
Issued in print and electronic formats.
ISBN 978-1-4597-1955-2 (pbk.).--ISBN 978-1-4597-1956-9 (pdf).--ISBN 978-1-4597-1957-6 (epub)

    1. Juvenile justice, Administration of--Canada. 2. Youth--Legal status, laws, etc.--Canada. I. Title.

KE9445.B39 2014   345.71'03   C2013-907407-4
KF9780.ZA2B39 2014   C2013-907408-2

1   2   3   4   5   18   17   16   15   14

We acknowledge the support of the **Canada Council for the Arts** and the **Ontario Arts Council** for our publishing program. We also acknowledge the financial support of the **Government of Canada** through the **Canada Book Fund** and **Livres Canada Books**, and the **Government of Ontario** through the **Ontario Book Publishing Tax Credit** and the **Ontario Media Development Corporation**.

Care has been taken to trace the ownership of copyright material used in this book. The author and the publisher welcome any information enabling them to rectify any references or credits in subsequent editions.

J. Kirk Howard, President

The publisher is not responsible for websites or their content unless they are owned by the publisher.

Printed and bound in Canada.

VISIT US AT

Dundurn.com | *@dundurnpress* | *Facebook.com/dundurnpress* | *Pinterest.com/dundurnpress*

Dundurn	Gazelle Book Services Limited	Dundurn
3 Church Street, Suite 500	White Cross Mills	2250 Military Road
Toronto, Ontario, Canada	High Town, Lancaster, England	Tonawanda, NY
M5E 1M2	L41 4XS	U.S.A. 14150

CONTENTS

ACKNOWLEDGEMENTS

First, I would like to acknowledge the Supreme Court of Canada. Over the decades, the membership of this nine-person Court has altered through retirement (mandatory at age seventy-five) or death. Increasingly, the Court has tried to hand down judgments that come ever closer to being decisions that can be read, understood, and discussed by those who want to be informed about the structure of our law, of our government, and more importantly, of our society's values. So, I thank — most profusely — the Supreme Court of Canada.

A second link in the chain between the law and the people is the media. It is possible, of course, in our highly computerized society to read the decisions of the Supreme Court of Canada online, but that can be an arduous process. On occasion, magazines such as *Maclean's* feature a particular subject for investigative reporting, in which the Supreme Court of Canada's judgments (such as those relating to tobacco) may form a part. Newspapers such as the *Toronto Star* may select a story reflecting a matter of social concern, such as bullying. And, on a daily basis, radio or television may briefly report on such stories.

The net effect of media reporting, at best, ranges from episodic to minimal. Perhaps the one constant to which we frequently refer in this series is the informed editorials in Canada's national newspaper, the *Globe and Mail*. Without hesitating, the *Globe and Mail* granted the right to reprint editorials (and there were many) on Supreme Court of Canada decisions. The approach of the *Globe and Mail* seems to be: Let the public be made aware. I thank them for their generosity and for maintaining consistently high standards.

Ordinarily, I would say that I take full responsibility for the contents of this book. Hopefully, however, the contents do not reflect my judgments but those of the Supreme Court of Canada. My task, as I saw it, was to discuss those judgments in a non-judgmental and accessible way.

INTRODUCTION

"It's the law!" What does that mean? If the law is "broken," especially the criminal law, then there may be a penalty, such as a fine or jail time, or community service, or conditional release. But who makes the law? Is it the government? How can a legislature draw clear lines, for example, in imposing individual responsibility?

Consider a fifteen-year-old victim of school bullying. He has "had enough." He takes his father's gun from a locked closet, loads it, and goes to school, where he shoots and seriously wounds one of his bullies. He is apprehended and charged. But how is he to be tried and, if found guilty, sentenced? Is he to be treated as a young offender or as an adult? If convicted, will he have a record that will follow him through high school and university, and into the job market? Is it really enough to say that a court will make the decisions?

The central issue explored in *Youth and the Law* is how a court makes such decisions. We will find that, like most laws intended to carry forward important public policy, those relating to young offenders significantly depend upon the courts to give such policy meaning in specific applications. Public policy has not varied for decades: protect and guide the young — and, at the same time, protect society. How is a court to interpret this policy in legal decisions? After all, isn't the only real meaning of the law how it is applied in specific cases?

The several thousand courts in Canada operate under certain principles or guidelines. A primary source of those principles is the Supreme Court of Canada. That is our jumping-off point: specific cases decided by that final arbiter, the Supreme Court of Canada. It may take five or more years for the Supreme Court to hear and decide an appeal. Yet, once the Supreme Court decides the case, it becomes the law. The majority decision of the nine justices of the Supreme Court is binding not only on the parties to the case, but on all people living in this country. The Court's ruling is the law of the land. It binds lower courts, legislatures, citizens, and residents of Canada. Only with considerable difficulty can a legislature overturn a Supreme Court ruling.

The Court generally does not make law; rather, it interprets the law in a specific case. In doing so, the lower court's findings are reviewed, and the Court then applies those findings to its own interpretation of the law. The parties to a case get an answer to their conflict: yes, no, or maybe. Sometimes the case is returned to the lower court for further proceedings on issues outlined but not resolved by the Court. For the most part, the parties are not interested in much else other than an answer.

The decision that is binding on the nation is how the Court explains itself — how it defines the issues and its reasoning in bringing them to conclusion. In this book, every effort has been made to present the Court's reasoning objectively and clearly. Readers will be given citations to access the Court's decisions online and will be left to critique judgments.

Let there be no doubt that public opinion can and does play a role in shaping law enforcement policy. Occasionally, if a Supreme Court decision is seen as moving too far from public acceptance, the government may decide that the decision should be clarified or redefined by new law. This is what happened when the Young

Offenders Act was recast as the Youth Criminal Justice Act, which exposes youth offenders to adult sentences.

Still, both the Court and the legislature must operate in the context of the Charter of Rights and Freedoms, part of the Constitution of Canada and, as such, the supreme law of the nation. This is partly what is meant by Canada being a nation of law. The Charter, enacted in 1982, can be seen as a firewall against popular sentiment. For example, the Charter tends to inhibit any government action that limits the rights of minority groups, such as the incarceration of Japanese-Canadians during the Second World War.

This book presents many case studies that focus on specific situations applied to the Charter. Through these decisions, we become aware of our responsibilities and our rights as citizens. And we see, as the Supreme Court must see, that process never ends. New cases, reflecting new facts, will continue to be presented, and their outcomes will be measured against the law, both constitutional and statutory.

WHO ARE THE JUDGES?

A few words must be said about the judges (or justices, as Supreme Court of Canada judges are called). Who are they? How are they chosen? How do they go about coming to decisions? The answer to these questions may help us better understand the decisions that we will be examining.

In 1989, Beverley McLachlin, then chief justice of British Columbia, received a telephone call from the prime minister of Canada. He asked if she would consider a new position: that of a justice of the Supreme Court of Canada.

It was within the power of the prime minister, accepted by his Cabinet, to offer the position. The appointment of a justice of the Supreme Court of Canada did not have to go through parliamentary committee or parliamentary consent, as such — a process enormously different from that of the United States where the president nominates and the Senate, following hearing, either gives the nomination a stamp of approval or rejection. (If the Senate rejects, then the candidacy of that person comes to an end.)

Justice McLachlin thanked the prime minister, accepted his offer, and became a justice of the Supreme Court of Canada. On January 7, 2000, the prime minister offered Justice McLachlin the position of chief justice of the Supreme Court, and she accepted.

There are nine justices who make up the Supreme Court of Canada. The conditions for their appointment are few, but they are important. They are appointed through the prime minister and the Governor in Council. In this regard, the "pool" for appointment by law is comprised of superior court judges or barristers with at least ten years in practice in a province or territory.

Once named to the Supreme Court, a justice cannot be removed from office so long as the justice carries out her/his duties in accordance with the law. But, at the age of seventy-five, there is forced retirement. (However, many retired justices are called back to serve in chairing special commissions.) A serving justice can only be removed from office for bad conduct or incapacity (such as illness).

By law, the prime minister is required to appoint three justices from Quebec. By tradition, the prime minister also appoints three justices from Ontario, two from the West, and one from Atlantic Canada.

How the prime minister goes about selecting a justice for the Supreme Court, given the broad limits described, is for the prime minister to determine. In 2012, Prime Minister Stephen Harper set new guidelines. He named a panel of five members of the House of Commons: three Conservatives (the prime minister's governing party), one New Democrat, and one Liberal. Their task was to review a list of qualified candidates put forward by the federal justice minister in consultation with the prime minister, the chief justice of the Supreme Court of Canada, the chief justice of

Quebec (where the next justice was to be selected), the Attorney General of Quebec, and provincial and territorial bar associations (as well as public suggestions).

The panel was instructed to submit a list of three recommended candidates — unranked — to the prime minister and he would select one from that list. A public hearing before a special parliamentary committee would be held before the prime minister finalized the appointment.

The first justice selected through the process described above was Richard Wagner, who was a long-time trial lawyer before becoming a justice of the Quebec Court of Appeal. In an interview with the *Globe and Mail*, Justice Wagner said, "I might surprise you, but I liked the [hearing] process. There is nothing to hide. I think a judge should follow the directions of society, and that means to explain to citizens what we do, how we do it, and why we do it. I think it's fair and it's reasonable."

A central concern, said Justice Wagner, is ensuring access to the justice system for all Canadians.

SOME FACTS

On the whole, it can be said that justices of the Supreme Court of Canada historically do not like to talk about themselves. But, there are some facts that may give rise to questions going to the makeup of the Court:

- There have been no persons "of colour" appointed to the Supreme Court of Canada.
- There have been no persons from among the "first peoples" (First Nations, Métis, and Inuit) appointed to the Supreme Court of Canada.

The fact is that white men, drawn from an elite part of the legal profession, constituted the "pool" from which justices of the Supreme

Court of Canada were drawn — at least until 1982. In that year — at the time the Charter of Rights and Freedoms, an important part of the Constitution of Canada, came into effect — the prime minister named the first woman to the Supreme Court: Bertha Wilson. She had emigrated to Canada with her husband John, a Presbyterian minister in Scotland, in 1949.

Justice Wilson had received an M.A. in philosophy at the University of Aberdeen. Once in Canada, she applied for admission to the law program at Dalhousie University in Halifax. She recalled an interview with the dean of the law school, and chuckled about it later. The dean advised her to "go home and take up crocheting." She didn't. She entered the Dalhousie law program in 1955 and was called to the Nova Scotia Bar after graduation.

In 1959, Justice Wilson moved to Toronto where she found employment with a leading law firm and later became head of research for that firm. Her job consisted in no small measure of writing opinions for members of the firm — a task that went a long way toward preparing her for work as a judge.

Justice Wilson received an invitation in 1979 to sit as a judge on the Ontario Court of Appeal. Her immediate response was surprise — and then laughter when, as a judge whose opinions reflected women's rights, she said, "I'll have to talk it over with my husband." She accepted the position on the Court of Appeal and served there until her appointment to the Supreme Court of Canada.

Justice Wilson was a Supreme Court justice from 1982 to 1991, retiring at the age of sixty-eight. There, she had an important role in interpreting the then newly-established Charter of Rights and Freedoms, including decisions relating to a woman's right to abortion (*R. v. Morgentaler* [1988] 1 *Supreme Court of Canada Reports* 30) and a spouse's right to claim self-defence to murder based on physical abuse by her/his spouse (called in law the battered wife syndrome) (*R. v. Lavallée* [1990] 1 *Supreme Court of Canada Reports* 852).

Since the appointment of Justice Wilson, a number of women have served as justices of the Supreme Court of Canada. In 2012, after serving as a justice for what she called ten "intense" years, Justice Marie Deschamps of Quebec resigned at the age of fifty-nine. (At that time, there were four women sitting as justices.) In an interview with CBC News a week after her resignation, Justice Deschamps was asked about "gender balance" of the Court. She answered, "I think every court should aim for half and half.... It's important that [the Court] is balanced.... I hope that the government will maintain at least four women on the Court. Whether the next candidate is a woman or it's the one that follows it will be for the government to decide."

In fact, the prime minister named Justice Richard Wagner of Quebec to the Court, thus lowering the number of women justices (at least for the time) to three.

It should be noted that the chief justice at the time of Justice Deschamps' resignation was Beverley McLachlin.

HOW ARE JUDGES TO DECIDE?

May emotion play a role in decision-making? For us, in reviewing decisions of the Supreme Court of Canada (or the decisions of any court, for that matter), an important question is whether justices can decide a case largely on the facts and the law as given. Can they remove (or largely isolate) any individual bias?

There are two parts to the answer — at least as applied to the Supreme Court of Canada:

1. No single justice decides a case. If the Court sits as a panel, there usually are seven justices who meet, discuss, and work toward an opinion that the chief justice usually assigns to a specific justice. If there is disagreement that cannot be otherwise resolved, then the way is open to a written dissent or a concurring opinion. (Often the justices are able to work out their disagreement to form a majority or a unanimous opinion.)

2. A case may be one that summons enormous emotion. Such was the case of Robert Latimer, a Saskatchewan farmer charged and convicted in the "mercy" killing of his disabled daughter. Twice the case went on appeal to the Supreme Court of Canada. The second time, the appeal was from a judgment of the Saskatchewan Court of Appeal that had increased a sentence of one year to ten years.

In a decision by the Court as a whole — not one attributed to any particular justice — the Supreme Court of Canada affirmed the judgment. The role of emotion in coming to decision was minimized.

Justice Ian Binnie, on his retirement after serving fourteen years on the Court, commented on the Latimer case in an extensive interview with Kirk Makin of the *Globe and Mail*:

> The Robert Latimer case was a hugely controversial case, but to me, the legal outcome was straightforward. You can't have people making their own judgments as to whether their child should live or die.
>
> In saying that, I make no moral judgment about what Latimer did. I accept his word that he did it because he thought it was best for his daughter.
>
> But the legal decision wasn't his to make. But the law is clear. When you talk about judges applying the law and not making it up, if the Criminal Code is clear about the penalty that follows from the crime of homicide, then that is the penalty that follows. You can't apply the law differently from case to case depending on a judge's personal view of whether a constitutional exemption is warranted.

So, there is no necessary correspondence between how much you agonize over a decision and what the moral implications or the controversy is outside the courtroom. My only function in that case is the right legal result. In that case the legal result was clear. My personal views of whether it was a good outcome or a bad outcome were irrelevant.

REFERENCES AND FURTHER READING

Fitzpatrick, Meagan. 2012. "Supreme Court Should Have Four Women Says Retiring Justice," *CBC.ca*, August 15.

Makin, Kirk. 2011. "Justice Ian Binnie's Exit Interview." *Globe and Mail*, September 23.

_____. 2012. "Supreme Court Judge Warns of 'Dangerous' Flaws in the System." *Globe and Mail*, December 12.

CHAPTER 1

PHYSICAL PUNISHMENT OF YOUTH — A CRIME?

Over the decades, the law has shielded young offenders from the full force of the criminal justice system. As reflected in statutes and court decisions, the law has long assumed that young people lack the maturity of adults and consequently are not to be held fully responsible for their actions. We can ask, at what age is a young person deemed in need of special protection and at what age does that protection end? Public policy states that, if at all possible, parents are to raise their children. The State intervenes only to support parents or those filling the role of parents, such as grandparents or other legal guardians.

We will begin our examination of young offenders' case studies with the subject of spanking. Criminal law is associated with punishment. Spanking is a form of corporal punishment. If we substitute the word *spanking* with *hitting* or *striking*, then we begin to see how it might be considered in setting public policy for young offenders. It can be used to define a "risk zone" — a danger zone in the sense that it may well bring the court to examine the lawfulness of what has been challenged.

In years gone by, it was usual for frustrated parents whose children seemed out of control to call upon the constable on the beat for assistance — to help their children conform with basic social behaviour. Modern life is more complex, but teachers and school principals still have wide discretion in shaping and enforcing rules for student conduct, including student and locker searches. Their power, however, is now subject to challenge. They may be questioned in court to prove that they acted reasonably. Students find that they have responsibilities and rights. For even as students, they are recognized as persons within the meaning of the Charter.

With most crimes, the first point of contact is the police. They investigate the incident and determine (perhaps in consultation with the Crown) whether charges will be laid. How do the police make decisions when the alleged wrongdoers are youths? How are youths to be questioned? Does the criminal process become more rigorous when the crime becomes more violent? Does the violent youthful offender lose the right to be treated as a youth in need of protection? This book will address such issues.

The range of penalties for adults violating the criminal law includes probation (often with conditions), prison, and possibly fines. All of these penalties are administered, directly or indirectly, by the State. In centuries past, the lash was part of criminal sentencing. In modern Canada, such corporal punishment is no longer used. Since individuals cannot legally assault others, the State cannot assault those who have violated its laws. Still, the State has allowed parents, teachers, or legal guardians to use force "by way of correction." How does this square with the Charter of Rights and Freedoms, part of the Constitution of Canada that, among other rights, affords all persons life, liberty, and security of the person? Among the questions raised in this chapter are:

- Does the criminal law of assault protect children as well as adults?
- Who may spank a child?
- What limits are there to physical force by adults against children?

The Criminal Code of Canada allows parents and teachers to use "reasonable force" to correct a child or pupil. This is an exception to the general criminal law, which prohibits anyone from striking another person without consent. The exception in section 43 of the Criminal Code provides: "Every school teacher, parent or person standing in the place of a parent is justified in using force by way of correction toward a pupil or child, as the case may be, who is under his care, if the force does not exceed what is reasonable under the circumstances."

THE FOUNDATION CASE

It was the constitutionality of this provision that was challenged by the Canadian Foundation for Children, Youth and the Law (the Foundation) on several grounds, all of which centred on the Charter. In light of the following points, the Foundation asked for a declaration that the defence to assault be set aside:

- The Foundation claimed that the exception violates section 7 of the Charter, which guarantees individuals against state action that infringes on life, liberty, or security of the person contrary to the principles of fundamental justice. This is done, for example, by a law that is too vague for there to be objective rules. (See the portion of the law quoted above.)
- Allowing the exception, said the Foundation, in effect gives state approval to cruel and unusual punishment in violation of section 12 of the Charter.
- Children are treated differently from adults. They are not given the same protections under the law, and this is a denial of their right to equal protection within the meaning of section 15(1) of the Charter.

The trial judge and the appellate court rejected the arguments of the Foundation. The matter came before the Supreme Court of Canada on June 6, 2003, and it was decided on January 30, 2004, in *Canadian Foundation for Children, Youth and the Law v. Attorney General of Canada* (the Foundation case). The Court permitted a number of public and private organizations, such as the Child Welfare League of Canada and the Ontario Association of Children's Aid Societies, to intervene in the case.

In a 6-3 vote (actually 7-2, considering the partial dissent of Justice Binnie, which approved the conclusion reached by the majority but not its reasoning), in the opinion given by Chief Justice Beverley McLachlin, the Court allowed the exception to the Criminal Code. But it listed a number of limitations on the use of the Criminal Code defence. The Court addressed such concerns as:

- Should force be denied against children of certain ages?
- Should the child's conduct be a measure of the kind of force that may be imposed?
- Should teachers and parents have an equal right to use force?

Three individual dissents to the majority opinion were given by Justices Louise Arbour, Marie Deschamps, and Binnie (the latter, as noted above, dissenting in part).

THE MAJORITY DECISION ON VAGUENESS

The primary issue considered by the Court majority in the Foundation case was whether section 43 was "vague or overbroad." Specifically, the Foundation argued that section 43 permitted violation of children's liberty and security by allowing parents and teachers the right to physically discipline them — so long as that discipline was deemed reasonable under the circumstances. The Foundation contended that discipline deemed reasonable under the circumstances is a vague concept. Thus, neither the accused nor the courts are able to have any firm fix on what is permitted and what is subject to criminal sanctions under section 43.

Chief Justice McLachlin, speaking for the Court majority, stated that a law need not provide certainty for it to be constitutional. It is enough for the law to set "an intelligible standard both for the citizens it governs and the officials who must enforce it." That standard is achieved if the law provides fair warning to potential wrongdoers that they may be entering an area of risk. The chief justice stated:

> A vague law prevents the citizen from realizing when he or she is entering an area of risk for criminal sanction. It similarly makes it difficult for law enforcement officers and judges to determine whether a crime has been committed. Yet, whether a law is vague may also depend on the judicial decisions which have interpreted it. Such decisions can add specific meaning to the statute.
>
> This invokes the further concern of putting too much discretion in the hands of law enforcement officials, and violates the precept that individuals should be governed by the rule of law, not the rule of persons. The doctrine of vagueness is directed generally at the evil of leaving basic policy matters to police officers, judges, and juries for resolution on an ad hoc [at the moment] and subjective basis, with the attendant dangers of arbitrary and discriminatory application.
>
> Ad hoc discretionary decision making must be distinguished from appropriate judicial interpretation. Judicial decisions may properly add

precision to a statute. Legislators can never foresee all the situations that may arise and, if they did, could not practically set them all out. It is thus in the nature of our legal system that areas of uncertainty exist and that judges clarify and augment the law on a case-by-case basis.

It follows that section 43 of the Criminal Code will satisfy the constitutional requirement for precision if it delineates a risk zone for criminal sanction. This achieves the essential task of providing general guidance for citizens and law enforcement officers.

This case illustrates that the courts may not be able to spell out with any precision the law in any particular case. What the Supreme Court can do, and what it has done, is indicate a danger area — an area of "risk." Those who approach it run the risk of crossing the line and having their actions deemed unconstitutional. Often the role of lawyers is to caution their clients that they run the risk of having their actions deemed unconstitutional and, with that declaration, being saddled by the Court with liability for the wrong done.

CREATING A RISK ZONE

To determine whether section 43 creates a risk zone, the Court majority considered the words of the provision in the context of their ordinary meaning, as well as court decisions interpreting those words.

The chief justice said that section 43 is precise as to who may access the provision: parents, teachers, and those standing in for parents in the sense of carrying all of their duties. In defence of section 43, the chief justice said that it requires that the force is used by way of correction. Further, that force must be reasonable under the circumstances. At this point, the chief justice turned to specific cases to provide further interpretation.

CORRECTION AND EDUCATION

The chief justice said of correction:

> First, the person applying the force must have intended it to be for educative or corrective purposes.... Accordingly, section 43 cannot [allow] outbursts of violence against a child motivated by anger or animated by frustration. It admits into its sphere of immunity only sober, reasoned uses of force that address the actual behaviour of the child and are designed to restrain, control, or express some symbolic disapproval of his or her behaviour. The purpose of the force must always be the education or discipline of the child....
>
> Second, the child must be capable of benefiting from the correction. This requires the capacity to learn and the possibility of successful correction. Force against children under two cannot be corrective, since on the evidence they are incapable of understanding why they are hit.... A child may also be incapable of learning from the application of force because of disability or some other contextual factor. In these cases, force will not be "corrective" and will not fall within the sphere of immunity provided by section 43.

REASONABLE UNDER THE CIRCUMSTANCES

Reasonableness, said the chief justice, is a concept long used in law in a number of different areas. It takes its meaning from particular facts and, in that regard, individuals have grown accustomed to measuring their conduct accordingly. The chief justice explained:

> The law has long used reasonableness to delineate areas of risk, without incurring the dangers of vagueness. The law of negligence, that has blossomed in recent decades to govern private actions in nearly all spheres of human activity, is founded upon the presumption that individuals are capable of governing their conduct in accordance with the standard of what is reasonable.
>
> But reasonableness as a guide to conduct is not confined to the law of negligence. The criminal law also relies on it. The Criminal Code [citing specific sections] expects that police officers will know what constitutes reasonable grounds for believing that an offence has been committed, such that an arrest can be made (section 495); that an individual will know what constitutes reasonable steps to obtain consent to sexual contact (section 273.2(b)); and that surgeons, in order to be exempted from criminal liability, will judge whether performing an operation is reasonable in all the circumstances of the case (section 45). These are merely a few examples; the criminal law is thick with the notion of reasonableness.

Again, while reasonableness is a standard that has been used to provide guidance, to signal approaching a zone of risk the Court emphasized that the factual and statutory context are important determiners as to meaning. The chief justice stated:

> Reality is that the term "reasonable" gives varying degrees of guidance, depending upon the

statutory and factual context. It does not insulate a law against a charge of vagueness. Nor, however, does it automatically mean that a law is void for vagueness. In each case, the question is whether the term, considered in light of principles of statutory interpretation and decided cases, delineates an area of risk and avoids the danger of arbitrary ad hoc law enforcement.

In the case of section 43, the chief justice said there were implicit limitations on the law that help shape its meaning, and she named the following:

1. Section 43 provides an exemption for the simple, non-consensual use of force. What it doesn't permit is force that causes harm or raises a reasonable prospect of harm. This means that section 43 can be used only in the mildest forms of assault. The chief justice wrote:

> Section 43 does not exempt from criminal sanction conduct that causes harm or raises a reasonable prospect of harm. It can be invoked only in cases of non-consensual application of force that results neither in harm nor in the prospect of bodily harm. This limits its operation to the mildest forms of assault. People must know that if their conduct raises an apprehension of bodily harm they cannot rely on section 43. Similarly, police officers and judges must know that the defence cannot be raised in such circumstances.

2. The line between mild discipline that does not cause harm and injuring a child in the name of discipline, the Court suggested, has been drawn in international treaties to which Canada is a party. As such, the Court cited cases requiring it to interpret Canadian statutes in a way that conforms with international treaties. The Court summarized those obligations as they relate to children: "Canada's international commitments confirm that physical correction that either harms or degrades a child is unreasonable."

The chief justice referred to specific treaties:

> Canada is a party to the United Nations Convention on the Rights of the Child. Article 5 of the Convention requires state parties to respect the responsibilities, rights and duties of parents or … other persons legally responsible for the child, to provide, in a manner consistent with the evolving capacities of the child, appropriate direction and guidance in the exercise by the child of the rights recognized in the present Convention.
>
> Article 19(1) requires the state party to protect the child from all forms of physical or mental violence, injury or abuse, neglect or negligent treatment, maltreatment or exploitation, including sexual abuse, while in the care of parent(s), legal guardian(s) or any other person who has the care of the child.
>
> Finally, Art. 37(a) requires [those nations agreeing to the Convention] to ensure that "no child shall be subjected to torture or other cruel, inhuman or degrading treatment or punishment." … This language is also found in the International Covenant on Civil and

Political Rights … to which Canada is a party. Article 7 of the Covenant states that "no one shall be subjected to torture or to cruel, inhuman or degrading treatment or punishment." The preamble to the International Covenant on Civil and Political Rights makes it clear that its provisions apply to "all members of the human family." From these international obligations, it follows that what is "reasonable under the circumstances" will seek to avoid harm to the child and will never include cruel, inhuman or degrading treatment.

3. Yet, the Court noted and emphasized that neither the Convention on the Rights of the Child nor the International Covenant on Civil and Political Rights explicitly require state parties to ban all corporal punishment of children.

4. A somewhat subtle approach has been taken in the interpretation of international treaties as applied to the corporal punishment of children by parents and teachers. Here the treaties have been read against section 7 of the Charter. In the process of monitoring compliance with the International Covenant on Civil and Political Rights, the Human Rights Committee of the United Nations has said that physical punishment of children in schools involves section 7's prohibition of degrading treatment or punishment. The committee, Chief Justice McLachlin noted, has not expressed a similar opinion regarding parental use of mild corporal punishment.

5. Further, objective consideration of what is "reasonable under the circumstances" in the case of child discipline, the chief justice said, comes from expert evidence that gives rise to "social consensus." Such an approach involves finding the

meaning of "reasonable under the circumstances" without any subjective interpretation by judges or police. The chief justice wrote:

> It is implicit in this technique that current social consensus on what is reasonable may be considered. It is wrong for caregivers or judges to apply their own subjective notions of what is reasonable. Section 43 demands an objective appraisal based on current learning and consensus. Substantial consensus, particularly when supported by expert evidence, can provide guidance and reduce the danger of arbitrary, subjective decision making.

CONCLUSIONS REACHED: REASONABLE UNDER THE CIRCUMSTANCES

The Court reached conclusions — based on interpretation and past decisions, as well as international treaties and "social consensus" — that were quite specific as to "reasonable under the circumstances" as set out in section 43. The chief justice stated these conclusions and they constitute the rules that now apply in the interpretation of section 43:

> Based on the evidence currently before the Court, there are significant areas of agreement among the experts on both sides of the issue....
> Corporal punishment of children under two years is harmful to them, and has no corrective value given the cognitive limitations of children under two years of age.

Corporal punishment of teenagers is harmful, because it can induce aggressive or antisocial behaviour.

Corporal punishment using objects, such as rulers or belts, is physically and emotionally harmful. Corporal punishment which involves slaps or blows to the head is harmful. These types of punishment, we may conclude, will not be reasonable.

Contemporary social consensus is that, while teachers may sometimes use corrective force to remove children from classrooms or secure compliance with instructions, the use of corporal punishment by teachers is not acceptable. Many school boards forbid the use of corporal punishment, and some provinces and territories have legislatively prohibited its use by teachers.... This consensus is consistent with Canada's international obligations, given the findings of the Human Rights Committee of the United Nations noted above. Section 43 will protect a teacher who uses reasonable, corrective force to restrain or remove a child in appropriate circumstances. Substantial societal consensus, supported by expert evidence and Canada's treaty obligations, indicates that corporal punishment by teachers is unreasonable.

A WORD ABOUT PRECEDENT

The chief justice acknowledged a critique by Justice Arbour (see "The Opinion of Justice Arbour" that follows). There have been a number of varied, even conflicting, decisions coming from trial and appellate Canadian courts as to the meaning of "reasonable under the circumstances" under section 43. Still, the chief justice said that the new guidelines should help to establish some more specific and objective principles that should lead to uniformity. (Justice Arbour did not dispute the conclusions reached by the majority. Rather, she insisted that those conclusions should have been developed under section 7 of the Charter and, more appropriately, through Parliamentary enactment of a new law.) The chief justice stated:

> It must be conceded at the outset that judicial decisions on section 43 in the past have sometimes been unclear and inconsistent, sending a muddled message as to what is and is not permitted. In many cases discussed by Arbour J., judges failed to acknowledge the [evolving] nature of the standard of reasonableness, and gave undue authority to outdated conceptions of reasonable correction.
>
> On occasion, judges erroneously applied their own subjective views on what constitutes reasonable discipline — views as varied as different judges' backgrounds. In addition, charges of assaultive discipline were seldom viewed as sufficiently serious to merit in-depth research and expert evidence or the appeals which might have permitted a unified national standard to emerge. However, the fact that a particular legislative term is open to varying interpretations by the courts is not fatal.... This case, and those that build on it, may permit a more uniform approach to "reasonable under the circumstances" than has prevailed in the past. Again, the issue is not whether section 43 has provided enough guidance in the past, but whether it expresses a standard

that can be given a core meaning in tune with contemporary consensus....

Precedent itself is not always crystal clear, the chief justice seemed to say. But, at least "precedent" should set a guiding principle as to how the law should be construed.

TRUMPING THE BEST INTERESTS OF THE CHILD PRINCIPLE

The law has overridden the principle of the best interests of the child. In the Foundation case, Chief Justice McLachlin, speaking for the Court, stated that the best interests of the child may be an important legal principle, but it can be overridden by other societal needs. The chief justice wrote:

> The legal principle of the "best interests of the child" may be subordinated to other concerns in appropriate contexts. For example, a person convicted of a crime may be sentenced to prison even where it may not be in his or her child's best interests. Society does not always deem it essential that the "best interests of the child" trump all other concerns in the administration of justice. The "best interests of the child," while an important legal principle and a factor for consideration in many contexts, is not vital or fundamental to our societal notion of justice, and hence is not a principle of fundamental justice.

YOU BE THE JUDGE

A MATTER OF CORRECTION?

THE FACTS

Under section 43 of the Criminal Code, Janet Wye, age twenty-five, was charged with assaulting her six-year-old son, Jason. Ms. Wye had taken Jason and her three-year-old daughter, Lucy, to the neighbourhood supermarket. Time and again that day, Ms. Wye had quietly and firmly told Jason not to tease his sister. And, time and again, Jason, who understood what he had been told, had proceeded to tease Lucy by pulling her hair and laughing at the result, namely, Lucy in tears with his mother visibly upset.

At the supermarket, Jason's teasing became more forceful. He not only pulled his sister's hair, but he yanked some of it out by the roots. Lucy screamed. Jason laughed, and he continued laughing — even when his mother screamed at him. Purposefully, Jason started teasing Lucy. He yanked as hard as he could at some of her long hair.

At that point, his visibly angry mother energetically shook Jason. She said to him, "How would you like it if someone pulled your hair?" She then reached down, took a small clump of Jason's hair, and pulled it out by the roots. Some blood flowed from the wound. Jason immediately stopped his teasing. Shocked, he looked at his mother and started to cry.

The store manager called the police. Ms. Wye was arrested and charged with assaulting Jason in violation of the Criminal Code. A Children's Aid worker took charge of the children.

THE ISSUE

Was the force Ms. Wye used against Jason intended to "correct" his behaviour and, as such, was it a defence against the assault charged?

POINTS TO CONSIDER

- Section 43 of the Criminal Code prohibits intentional use of force against another without that person's consent.
- The force that Ms. Wye used against Jason was not minor. It was not what the law would term *de minimis*.
- Section 43 does indeed provide a defence against assault of a child by a parent or schoolteacher if it is intended for correction and/or educational purpose.
- A section 43 defence by a parent must demonstrate that the assault was reasonable under the circumstances.
- The child assaulted (Jason) must be capable of benefiting from the discipline, that is, the assault.

DISCUSSION

Ms. Wye's defence would likely be rejected for two reasons: (1) the force she used was not imposed to educate or correct Jason's behaviour, (2) under the circumstances, the Court would conclude that it was not "reasonable."

TO CORRECT AND EDUCATE

On the facts, Ms. Wye physically disciplined her child while she was angry. The chief justice, speaking for the Supreme Court of Canada in the Foundation case, stated that it is not possible for a person in a state of anger to administer physical discipline which, if it is used at all, must be for educative or corrective purposes. She wrote:

> The person applying the force must have intended it to be for educative or corrective purposes.... Accordingly, section 43 cannot exculpate [allow] outbursts of violence against a child motivated by anger or animated by frustration. It admits into its sphere of immunity only sober, reasoned uses of force that address the actual behaviour of the child and are designed to restrain, control or express some symbolic disapproval of his or her behaviour. The purpose of the force must always be the education or discipline of the child....

REASONABLE UNDER THE CIRCUMSTANCES

An important element for a section 43 defence, the Court ruled, is that the physical discipline must be reasonable under the circumstances. The Foundation questioned whether this test has any objectivity, and whether what is "reasonable" is open to the trial judge's interpretation. So it was that the Foundation cited *The Queen v. K.(M.)* (1992), 74 *Canadian Criminal Cases*, 3d series 108. There, Justice O'Sullivan of the Manitoba Court of Appeal wrote, "The discipline administered to the boy in question in these proceedings [a kick in the rear] was mild indeed compared to the discipline I received in my home."

Reasonableness, said Chief Justice McLachlin in the Foundation case, is a broad standard. But it does have meaning. Trial judges are not free to do whatever they want. There are limits placed on its application. The chief justice wrote:

> The reality is that the term reasonable gives varying degrees of guidance, depending upon the statutory and factual context. [In itself, the term] does not insulate a law against a charge of vagueness. Nor, however, does it automatically mean that a law is void for vagueness. In each case, the question is whether the term, considered in light of principles of statutory interpretation and decided cases, delineates an area of risk and avoids the danger of arbitrary ad hoc [individual] law enforcement.

> Is section 43's reliance on reasonableness, considered in this way, unconstitutionally vague? Does it indicate what conduct risks criminal sanction and provide a principled basis for enforcement? While the words on their face are broad, a number of implicit limitations add precision.

> The first limitation arises from the behaviour for which section 43 provides an exemption, simple non-consensual application of force. Section 43 does not exempt from criminal sanction conduct

that causes harm or raises a reasonable prospect of harm. It can be invoked only in cases of non-consensual application of force that results neither in harm nor in the prospect of bodily harm. This limits its operation to the mildest forms of assault. People must know that if their conduct raises an apprehension of bodily harm they cannot rely on section 43. Similarly, police officers and judges must know that the defence cannot be raised in such circumstances.

Applied to Ms. Wye, her section 43 defence would likely fail. She struck in anger, and this probably foreclosed an intent to be corrective. Yet more to the point, she caused bodily harm to Jason. She yanked out his hair and caused him to bleed.

A CASE OF SERIOUS MISBEHAVIOUR

Penny Franklin, age twelve, understood the difference between right and wrong. However, she was the leader of a gang of seven girls who called themselves the Holy Terrors. The object of the gang was to intimidate neighbourhood girls who were the same age or younger.

Penny's parents believed in the philosophy of "spare the rod and spoil the child." Learning of their daughter's involvement with the gang, they cautioned her in the strongest possible terms to stop, and they spoke with school authorities — all to no avail.

One day, Mr. and Mrs. Franklin became aware of a particularly vicious attack by the Holy Terrors on eleven-year-old Zoë. No one struck Zoë, but for more than an hour she was swarmed by the Holy Terrors and intimidated. To Penny's parents, particularly in view of the warning they had given their daughter, this was extremely serious misbehaviour. They felt strongly that it was their duty as parents to take corrective action. Mrs. Franklin took responsibility for meting out discipline. She strapped her daughter, giving her ten strong lashes on her bottom. The punishment left bruises on the girl.

Penny's serious misbehaviour, however, is not a factor in determining whether her mother's use of the strap was justified. Corporal punishment, said Chief Justice McLachlin for the Court majority in the Foundation case, should be used only to correct, never to punish. She wrote, "It is improper to … focus on the gravity of a child's wrongdoing, which invites a punitive rather than corrective focus.… The focus under section 43 is on the correction of the child, not on the gravity of the precipitating event. Obviously, force employed in the absence of any behaviour requiring correction by definition cannot be corrective." Further, discipline cannot be inflicted if it is likely to cause harm to the child.

CHALLENGE QUESTION

SETTING STANDARDS

Q: Will the "rules" set by the Supreme Court in the Foundation case remain fixed? For example, if it is wrong to spank a teenager today, might it become acceptable at another time?

The Court ruled that objective standards should always apply. Further, central to such objective standards is that corporal discipline should always be directed toward correction and/or education.

Trial judges must decide what is reasonable under the circumstances and at the same time recognize that circumstances may change over time. The Court suggested that an approach might be to look to expert evidence, though it did not expressly state that it might come from child psychologists or social workers. Chief Justice McLachlin stated:

> Determining what is reasonable under the circumstances in the case of child discipline is also assisted by social consensus and expert evidence on what constitutes reasonable corrective discipline. The criminal law often uses the concept of reasonableness to accommodate evolving mores and avoid successive "fine-tuning" amendments. It is implicit in this technique that current social consensus on what is reasonable may be considered.
>
> It is wrong for caregivers or judges to apply their own subjective notions of what is reasonable. Section 43 demands an objective appraisal based on current learning and consensus. Substantial consensus, particularly when supported by expert evidence, can provide guidance and reduce the danger of arbitrary, subjective decision making.

JUSTICE BINNIE'S PARTIAL DISSENT
IN THE FOUNDATION CASE

Justice Binnie agreed with the Court's result as applied to parents and those standing in for parents. He had this to say about the proper role of the appellate courts in "calibrating" the application of rules to changing societal values:

> Providing a defence to a criminal prosecution in the circumstances stated in section 43 is rationally connected to the objective of limiting the intrusion of the Criminal Code into family life.
>
> As to minimal impairment, the wording of section 43 not only permits calibration of the immunity to different circumstances and children of different ages, but it allows for adjustment over time. In this respect, the Crown's expert, Nicholas Bala, stated:
>
> > In the past, the use of belts, straps, rulers, sticks and other similar objects to deliver a punishment was commonly accepted, both by society and the courts, as reasonable in the chastisement of children. Today, most courts hold that, in most circumstances, the use of these objects is excessive. As well, previously, courts have considered punishment causing temporary pain lasting a few days, but without permanent injury, to be reasonable. Today's courts scrutinize the level of pain, bruises, red marks and other signs of temporary harm carefully. In most cases, when they find that a child has suffered some injury, the

teacher, parent or person taking the place
of a parent is convicted of assault.

In the past, as Arbour J. demonstrates in
her reasons, the elasticity of section 43 has led
to acquittals in some quite shocking circumstances. However, in my view, it is the function
of the appellate courts to rein in overly elastic
interpretations that undermine the limited purpose of section 43, which is what the interpretive
guidance offered by the chief justice is designed
to do, provided the courts stop short of judicial
amendment [of the statutory law].

THE MEDIA'S RESPONSE

The *Globe and Mail* commented on the Court's decision in the
Foundation case:

In upholding the legality of mild spankings yesterday, the Supreme Court of Canada recognized
that the protection of children also requires protection of their families from the State. But that
was the status quo — and some judges have in
the past made questionable decisions that left
children unprotected from abuse. (A Manitoba
appeal court judge once allowed a kick in the
rear, saying that he had suffered worse as a child.)
So the court wisely drew a line between the mild
spanking and the abusive one.

It is not easy to define the boundary between
reasonable force to correct a child's behaviour and
abusive force that harms a child. The 7-2 judgment

will not, alas, provide perfect protection for all children. Many instances of corporal punishment will remain at the borderline of what is legal, and of what most Canadians would consider tolerable. Most people have seen assaultive behaviour — a twist to the wrist or the cartilage of an ear, a slap to the back of the neck, a series of hard blows to a small child's back — engaged in by other people in public, or perhaps by themselves at home after a sleepless night. It will remain for the lower courts to define the boundary more precisely, using the Supreme Court's guidelines. [Here follows a summary of the Court's guidelines.]

No one should read the [Court's] judgment as a kind of official sanction for hitting children. Rather, the ruling recognizes what Chief Justice Beverley McLachlin called the "blunt hand of the criminal law" should not be brought down on families, except as a last resort, lest it harm the children in doing so.

A couple of generations ago, it was not uncommon for parents to use belts, straps or sticks on their children. A generation ago, it was permissible to strike children hard enough to leave them in pain for a few days; that is no longer permitted. Yesterday's ruling, by narrowing the definition of reasonable force, marks a small but important step in society's advance ("Spanking Is Permitted, but Mind the New Rules" 2004).

ANOTHER POINT OF VIEW

Globe and Mail columnist Margaret Wente also commented on the Court's decision regarding spanking:

Anti-spankers pretend that little children are rational beings, like the rest of us, and that disciplinary measures should be designed to make them "think." Actually, little children are more like puppies, most of which are innately loving and aim to please, but need to internalize the norms of civilized conduct. Brute force is a last resort, but sometimes a smack with a rolled-up newspaper wouldn't hurt. In fact, the principles of training dogs and training children are more or less the same, and it strikes me that if parents were required to attend dog-training courses, we'd all be a whole lot better off. There's nothing worse than being around a dog that's got its owner cowed, unless it's being around an eight-year-old who likes to scream, "You're not the boss of me!"

In a culture that has elevated violence against children to the greatest of all human evils (and redefined violence to include just about everything), the harm that spanking does has been ridiculously exaggerated. [Some of] the happiest and most grounded kids I've ever met belong to families that believe in physical discipline. I know equally splendid kids whose parents never laid a finger on them. It's not the spanks or lack of them that matter. It's the clear expectations, the consistency, the ability to set boundaries, the time their parents spend with them, and the steady love. The best parents I know are the ones who spend great amounts of time attending — really attending — to their children. They put in the mileage, and there's no substitute for it (Wente 2004).

CHALLENGE QUESTION

ARE CHILDREN EQUAL
BEFORE AND UNDER THE LAW?

Q: *Does section 43 of the Criminal Code offend section 15 of the Charter?*

Here is the context for this question:

- The Charter is part of the Constitution of Canada, and as such it is the supreme law of the land. No statute can stand if it offends the Charter.
- Section 15(1) of the Charter provides for equality rights with these words: "Every individual is equal before and under the law and has the right to equal protection and equal benefit of the law without discrimination and, in particular, without discrimination based on race, national or ethnic origin, colour, religion, sex, age, or mental or physical disability."
- A violation of section 15 of the Charter can be excused if it meets the terms of section 1 of the Charter, which provides: "The Canadian Charter of Rights and Freedoms guarantees the rights and freedoms set out in it subject only to such reasonable limits prescribed by law as can be demonstrably justified in a free and democratic society."

The Foundation argued that section 43 decriminalizes the offence of assault against children. As such, a message is sent that a child is less worthy of recognition or value as a human being, or as a member of Canadian society.

Chief Justice McLachlin, for the Court, rejected the argument. There is a difference between the Charter requirement of equal treatment and identical treatment. That Parliament chose section 43 reflects its desire to protect the need of children for safety and security "in an age-appropriate manner." She wrote:

> The difficulty with this argument [that of the Foundation], as we shall see, is that it equates equal treatment with identical treatment, a proposition which our jurisprudence has consistently rejected. In fact, declining to bring the blunt hand of the criminal law down on minor disciplinary contacts ... reflects the resultant impact this would have on the interests of the child and on family and school relationships. Parliament's choice not to criminalize this conduct does not devalue or discriminate against children, but responds to the reality of their lives by addressing their need for safety and security in an age-appropriate manner....
>
> Children need to be protected from abusive treatment. They are vulnerable members of Canadian society and Parliament and the Executive act admirably when they shield children from psychological and physical harm. In so acting, the government responds to the critical need of all children for a safe

environment. Yet this is not the only need of children. Children also depend on parents and teachers for guidance and discipline, to protect them from harm and to promote their healthy development within society. A stable and secure family and school setting is essential to this growth process.

Section 43 is Parliament's attempt to accommodate both of these needs. It provides parents and teachers with the ability to carry out the reasonable education of the child without the threat of sanction by the criminal law.

The criminal law will decisively condemn and punish force that harms children, is part of a pattern of abuse, or is simply the angry or frustrated imposition of violence against children; in this way, by decriminalizing only minimal force of transient or trivial impact, section 43 is sensitive to children's need for a safe environment. But section 43 also ensures the criminal law will not be used where the force is part of a genuine effort to educate the child, poses no reasonable risk of harm that is more than transitory and trifling, and is reasonable under the circumstances. Introducing the criminal law into children's families and educational environments in such circumstances would harm children more than help them. So Parliament has decided not to do so, preferring the approach of educating parents against physical discipline.

This decision, far from ignoring the reality of children's lives, is grounded in their lived experience. The criminal law is the most powerful tool at Parliament's disposal. Yet it is a blunt instrument whose power can also be destructive of family and educational relationships....

I am satisfied that a reasonable person acting on behalf of a child, apprised of the harms of criminalization that section 43 avoids, the presence of other governmental initiatives to reduce the use of corporal punishment, and the fact that abusive and harmful conduct is still prohibited by the criminal law, would not conclude that the child's dignity has been offended in the manner contemplated by section 15(1).

Children often feel a sense of disempowerment and vulnerability; this reality must be considered when assessing the impact of section 43 on a child's sense of dignity. Yet, as emphasized, the force permitted is limited and must be set against the reality of a child's mother or father being charged and pulled into the criminal justice system, with its attendant rupture of the family setting, or a teacher being detained pending bail, with the inevitable harm to the child's crucial educative setting. Section 43 is not arbitrarily demeaning. It does not discriminate. Rather, it is firmly grounded in the actual needs and circumstances of children. I conclude that section 43 does not offend section 15(1) of the Charter.

On the point denying the application of section 15 of the Charter, Chief Justice McLachlin spoke for a majority of six. Justices Binnie and Deschamps dissented; they would have allowed children the protection of section 15. Justice Binnie would have permitted the conclusion reached by the Court majority, but only after the Crown demonstrated justification for the restraint. Justice Deschamps would have afforded children protection and she would have rejected the government's claim of justification. Justice Arbour saw no need to deal with section 15. Her reason: section 43 offended section 7 of the Charter. We will briefly set out the reasoning of Justices Binnie and Deschamps.

JUSTICE BINNIE'S PARTIAL DISSENT ON SECTION 43

Quoting the majority opinion, Justice Binnie said: "It may be that introducing the criminal law into children's families and educational environments [in the context of section 43] would harm children more than help them." But, he stated, this is a reason that goes toward justifying the action of government within the meaning of section 15 of the Charter. It does not speak to whether children are protected within the meaning of section 15.

Justice Binnie then addressed himself to whether corrective force by parents might be justified. He concluded, "To deny children the ability to have their parents, or persons standing in their parents' place, to be successfully prosecuted for reasonable corrective force under the Criminal Code does not leave them without effective recourse. It just helps to keep the family out of the criminal courts. In my view, section 43 in relation to parents and persons standing in their place is justified on this basis."

However, Justice Binnie could not find the same justification as applied to teachers. He wrote:

> The question is whether the undoubted need to keep order in schools justifies the section 43 exemption of teachers from the assault provisions of the Criminal Code.
>
> The Law Reform Commission of Canada recommended the repeal of the section 43 defence for school teachers, stating that the ultimate sanction should be the removal of a child from school, not corporal punishment: Law Reform Commission of Canada, Working Paper 38, Assault (1984), at p. 44. A number of countries have abolished or modified similar legislative immunities for teachers: see, e.g., section 47 of the British Education (No. 2) Act 1986 (U.K.), 1986, c. 61; section 59 of the New Zealand Crimes Act 1961 (N.Z.), 1961/43; and s. 139A of the New Zealand Education Act 1989 (N.Z.), 1989/80.
>
> While I accept that order in the schools is a legitimate objective, I do not think that giving non-family members an immunity for the criminal assault of children "by way of correction" is a reasonable or proportionate legislative response to that problem. The attempt to save the constitutionality of section 43 by rewriting it to distinguish between parents and teachers and carving out school order from the more general subject matter of "correction" is, in my view, a job for Parliament. In short, section 43 does not

minimally impair the child's equality right, and is not a proportionate response to the problem of order in the schools.

THE DISSENT OF JUSTICE DESCHAMPS

Justice Deschamps said that section 43 should be interpreted according to the intent of the Parliament at the time of the law's enactment. As such, the constraints that the majority imposed on section 43 go too far. The Court majority, Justice Deschamps said, has inserted its views as to what the law should be rather than the clear intent of the Parliament. In this regard, she cited and approved the reasoning of Justice Arbour, which is set out (below) in "The Opinion of Justice Arbour."

Justice Deschamps then proceeded to discuss the application of section 15 of the Charter to children, who, she said, have long been recognized as a vulnerable group in need of protection. She wrote:

> Children as a group face pre-existing disadvantage in our society. They have been recognized as a vulnerable group time and again by legislatures and courts. Historically, their vulnerability was entrenched by the traditional legal treatment of children as the property or chattel of their parents or guardians. Fortunately, this attitude has changed in modern times with a recognition that children, as individuals, have rights, including the right to have their security and safety protected by their parents, families and society at large. This recognition is illustrated by several decisions of this Court (see, e.g., *B. (R.) v. Children's Aid Society of Metropolitan Toronto*, (1995) 1 *Supreme Court of Canada Reports* 315; *Winnipeg Child*

and Family Services v. K.L.W., (2000) 2 *Supreme Court of Canada Reports* 519); ... by government policy and laws (for example, specific criminal law protections, family law reforms, and child protection services), and by international legal authorities....

However, by permitting incursions on children's bodies by their parents or teachers, section 43 appears to be a throwback to old notions of children as property. Section 43 reinforces and compounds children's vulnerability and disadvantage by withdrawing the protection of the criminal law. Moreover, because the accused is the very person most often charged with the control and trusteeship of the child, being deprived of the legal protection to which everyone else is presumptively entitled exacerbates the already vulnerable position of children. The entitlement to protection is derived by virtue of our status as persons and the status of children as persons deserves equal recognition....

[Section] 43 as it currently stands permits a broader range of assaults to be justified by its terms. There is a general consensus among experts that the only benefit of mild to moderate uses of force, such as spanking, is short-term compliance. Anything more serious is not only not conducive to furthering the education of children, but also potentially harmful to their development and health.... It cannot be seriously argued that children need corporal punishment to grow and learn. Indeed, their capacities and circumstances would generally point in the opposite direction — that they can learn through reason and example while feeling secure in their physical safety and bodily integrity.

By condoning assaults on children by their parents or teachers, section 43 perpetuates the notion of children as property rather than human beings and sends the message that their bodily integrity and physical security is to be sacrificed to the will of their parents, however misguided.... Section 43 creates a category of "second-class citizens" that must suffer a "consequent attenuation of [their] right to dignity and physical security." Far from corresponding to the actual needs and circumstances of children, section 43 compounds the pre-existing disadvantage of children as a vulnerable and often-powerless group whose access to legal redress is already restricted.

The Charter infringement in this case is discriminatory at a very direct and basic level. It clearly impairs the equal rights of children to bodily integrity and security in a much more intrusive way than necessary to achieve a valid legislative objective. The provincial and policy mechanisms available do not change this effect.

THE OPINION OF JUSTICE ARBOUR

Justice Arbour came to a conclusion, in her words, "not very different from that reached by the chief justice." The majority reached their conclusions as to the limitations of corrective force in section 43 because they reflected what the statute, itself, requires. Justice Arbour reached her conclusions as to these limitations because they reflect what the Charter, as part of the supreme law of the land, requires. For that reason, because section 43 offends the Charter, Justice Arbour would have set aside the statute. To do so, she said, does not leave either parents or teachers defenceless in appropriate cases. She pointed to two common law defences, which are described below in "You Be the Judge: A Case of Necessity?" and "Still Another Common Law Defence: *De Minimis?*"

Further, and this is central to Justice Arbour's argument, it should be Parliament that brings its laws into conformity with the Charter. It is not the Court's role to reshape the law to meet the requirements of the Charter.

SECTION 43 OF THE CRIMINAL CODE

Section 43 has long been part of the criminal law. As such, Justice Arbour said, it stood for values allowing "reasonable" force on children. She stated:

> That section 43 is rooted in an era where deploying "reasonable" violence was an accepted technique in the maintenance of hierarchies in the family and in society is of little doubt. Children remain the only group of citizens who are deprived of the protection of the criminal law in relation to the use of force....
>
> Whether such policy ought to be acceptable today with respect to children is the subject of ongoing debate in society about the appropriateness and effectiveness of the use of corporal punishment by way of correction. We have not been asked to take a side in that debate. However, the issue is also the subject of the constitutional challenge brought before us by the Foundation. This legal challenge is what we must address.

SECTION 7 OF THE CHARTER

To Justice Arbour, it is section 7 of the Charter that must be examined to determine the constitutionality of section 43. Section 7 provides: "Everyone has the right to life, liberty and security of the person, and the right not to be deprived thereof except in accordance with the principles of fundamental justice."

The first part of the test under section 7 is whether section 43 affects the "security of the person" when the person is a child. Justice Arbour said there is no doubt on this point. The criminal law is an important means by which the State protects the liberty and security of its citizens. The operation of section 43 withdraws that security, which applies to parents and teachers, from children.

This brought Justice Arbour to the second part of the analysis of section 7: Has the security of children been denied by section 43 in accordance with the principles of fundamental justice? In this regard, she accepted the argument of the Foundation that "reasonable under the circumstances" is a standard too vague to allow for clear guidelines; judges could do as they pleased. And, in the view of Justice Arbour, that is precisely what many courts have done. There were no objective case guides (precedents).

It may be, Justice Arbour said, that "reasonableness" in other contexts does permit objective standards. For example, there is something to measure the standard of reasonableness against if the question relates to self-defence. In the face of a defined threat, what was necessary to defend oneself? But, the same may not be said of "reasonableness" applied to the physical discipline of children. Justice Arbour wrote:

> This is not so in the case of corporal punishment of children, where there is no built-in [relationship] between physical punishment and bad behaviour that can be used to assess proportionality. Indeed, the chief justice concludes ... that

the gravity of the child's conduct is not a "relevant contextual consideration" as it invites a punitive, rather than a corrective focus.

Corporal punishment is a controversial social issue. Conceptions of what is "reasonable" in terms of the discipline of children, whether physical or otherwise, vary widely, and often [involve] cultural and religious beliefs as well as political and ethical ones. Such conceptions are intertwined with how other controversial issues are understood, including the relationship between the State and the family and the relationship between the rights of the parent and the rights of the child.

Whether a person considers an instance of child corporal punishment "reasonable" may depend in large part on his or her own parenting style and experiences. While it may work well in other contexts, in this one the term "reasonable force" has proven not to be a workable standard. Lack of clarity is particularly problematic here because the rights of children are engaged....

Justice Arbour stated that because reasonable under the circumstances is vague, neither parents nor teachers understand the zone of risk, the area in which they might be charged under the criminal law: "A standardless sweep does not become acceptable simply because it results from the whims of judges and justices of the peace rather than the whims of law enforcement officials. Cloaking whims in judicial robes [is] not sufficient to satisfy the principles of fundamental justice."

Justice Arbour further ruled, that because section 43 is "standardless" — that is, too vague — it cannot meet that portion of section 1 of the Charter, that might otherwise allow a violation of section 7 to stand.

INTERNATIONAL TREATIES AND CANADA: PROTECTION OF THE CHILD

Section 43, Justice Arbour said, had to be measured against the requirements of the Charter, and especially section 7 of that document. After all, the Charter, as the highest law in Canada, sets standards that must be met by statutes such as the Criminal Code.

A source for understanding the rights of children, as they relate to principles of fundamental justice within the meaning of section 7, are Canada's international obligations found in treaties. There, said Justice Arbour, Canada not only has obligated itself to the United Nations Convention on the Rights of the Child, but Canada is also committed to take part in the Committee on the Rights of the Child, set up under the agreement. That committee, whose comments are not binding, said of section 43 in a summary given by Justice Arbour:

> It is notable that the Committee has not recommended clarifying these laws [section 43] so much as abolishing them entirely.... The Committee's Concluding Observations on Canada's First Report are illustrative:
>
> > Penal legislation allowing corporal punishment of children by parents, in schools and in institutions where children may be placed [should be considered for review]. In this regard ... physical punishment of children in families [should] be prohibited. In connection with the child's right to physical integrity ... and in the light of the best interests of the child, ... the possibility of introducing new legislation and follow-up mechanisms to prevent

violence within the family [should be considered], and ... educational campaigns [should] be launched with a view to changing attitudes in society on the use of physical punishment in the family and fostering the acceptance of its legal prohibition. Committee on the Rights of the Child, Report adopted by the Committee at its 233rd meeting on 9 June 1995, Ninth Session, CRC/C/43, at para. 93.

In its most recent Concluding Observations, the Committee expressed "deep concern" that Canada had taken "no action to remove section 43 of the Criminal Code" and recommended the adoption of legislation to remove the existing authorization of the use of "reasonable force" in disciplining children and explicitly prohibit all forms of violence against children, however light, within the family, in schools and in other institutions where children may be placed. (Committee on the Rights of the Child 2003, paras. 32–33)

YOU BE THE JUDGE

A CASE OF NECESSITY?

THE FACTS

Simon Just has been an elementary school teacher for fifteen years. He is recognized by school administrators and students as fair-minded but strict. Rules of conduct, he has frequently said, are meant to be followed. "If they are not taught here and accepted, the likelihood is that they will not be accepted later on in a child's education."

Simon Just is an athletic person with a black belt in karate.

One day, he heard screaming in the school hall. Two ten-year-old boys were in the midst of a fight. Both had drawn knives and they were slashing at each other. Both were bleeding.

Just rushed over. He knew both boys. He had been their teacher for three years, and he considered them "hot heads." They had little capacity to manage their frustrations. With two swift karate chops, Just not only disabled both boys, but knocked them out. Both were rushed to the hospital. They suffered from concussions and dislocated shoulders.

The police laid charges of assault against Just, who admitted that shouting at the boys during the fight might have ended the confrontation. But he felt that this was a chance that he simply could not take. In his view, the boys had been dangerous, capable of seriously wounding him and each other with their knives.

THE ISSUE

Did the fight present an emergency situation that justified Just's assault?

POINTS TO CONSIDER

- Section 43 of the Criminal Code provides: "Every schoolteacher, parent or person standing in the place of a parent is justified in using

force by way of correction toward a pupil or
child, as the case may be, who is under his care,
if force does not exceed what is reasonable
under the circumstances."

- In the context of section 43, teachers may
reasonably apply force to remove a child
from a classroom or secure compliance with
instructions, but force cannot be used merely
as corporal punishment.

- Section 8(3) of the Criminal Code allows for
the common law defence of necessity. This
defence recognizes that there are emergency
situations where the law does not hold people
accountable if they act in self-defence or to
save others.

- In effect, the defence of necessity is an excuse,
not a justification for violating the law.

DISCUSSION

If the reasoning of Justice Arbour in her Foundation case
dissent was accepted, Simon Just might have a valid defence
within the meaning of section 8(3) of the Criminal Code. He
acted to protect children from seriously wounding or possibly killing each other. They were slashing at each other with
knives. Both were bleeding. They were known in the school as
"hot heads." Indeed, the fight took place in the school where
Just was a teacher. He saw the fight and acted instantly.

Was there a reasonable alternative to the assault, to the
use of karate which caused injury? If such an alternative
existed, then, under the defence of necessity, he was obligated
to use it. Just seemed aware that the law did not approve of

the use of force. His alternative was to yell at the boys to stop fighting. However, Just felt that he could not take the chance that the boys would not stop fighting on his command. He believed he had to act quickly to end the fight.

Once Just put before the trial court sufficient evidence to raise the issue of necessity, then the burden was on the Crown to show that the defence was invalid beyond a reasonable doubt.

MORE ON JUSTICE ARBOUR'S REASONING

The Court majority in the Foundation case did not discuss the necessity defence. The issue before the Court, after all, was the Charter challenge to section 43 of the Criminal Code. Justice Arbour took a broader view. She did so in the context of her conclusion that the Charter required that section 43 be set aside.

The defence of necessity, she emphasized, is a long-standing common law rule incorporated into section 8(3) of the Criminal Code and recognized by the Court in *Perka v. The Queen*, [1984] 2 *Supreme Court of Canada Reports* 232. Justice Arbour wrote:

> I see no reason why, if the above requirements are met, the defence of necessity would not be available to parents and teachers should they intervene to protect children from themselves or others. Other authors have also proposed the use of necessity for parents and teachers should the section 43 defence be abolished. (See, Anne McGillivray, "He'll Learn It on His Body: Disciplining Childhood in Canadian Law,"

International Journal of Children's Rights
193, at p. 240.)

In *The Queen v. Morris* (1981), 61
Canadian Criminal Cases (2d series) 163
(Alberta Queen's Bench), the defence of
necessity succeeded in absolving a husband on a charge of common assault of
his wife. The husband had restrained his
inebriated wife when she tried to jump out
of their truck. The husband honestly and
reasonably believed that the intervention
was necessary. The judge noted, at p. 166,
that: "To have allowed his wife to get out
of the truck to walk on a dark road in an
intoxicated condition would have shown
wanton or reckless disregard for her life or
safety and could have constituted criminal
negligence on his part...."

If a parent were to forcibly restrain
a child in order to ensure that the child
complied with a doctor's instructions to
receive a needle, section 43 would be of
no assistance to excuse the use of restraint,
but the parent would, in my view, have the
common law defence of necessity available
to him or her should a charge of assault
be pursued. The common law defence
of necessity has always been available to
parents in appropriate circumstances and
would continue to be available if the section 43 defence were struck down.

> Common sense under a test of reasonableness seems to be the direction taken by Justice Arbour. For example, parents will be seen as justified in restraining an unruly child who insists on crossing the street on a red light. The parent is acting largely for the purpose of the safety of the child.

STILL ANOTHER COMMON LAW DEFENCE: *DE MINIMIS*?

Police and prosecutors, in effect, screen all criminal charges. They can and do determine, from the start, which charges will proceed to court. Challenging their discretion not to press a charge is seldom possible. Yet, suppose a charge is brought that the accused believes is trivial. Can a defence be mounted on that basis alone?

Justice Arbour argued that in situations where there has been a "technical" violation of the law against assault, a court is free to dismiss the case (to stay proceedings) on the ground that the breach was only "trivial." In this regard, Justice Arbour cited the legal axiom in Latin: *de minimis non curat lex* — or, loosely translated, "The law does not concern itself with trifles."

RAISING THE *DE MINIMIS* DEFENCE

According to Justice Arbour, the cases supporting the *de minimis* rule in criminal cases are "unsatisfactory." Yet the fact remains that it has been used a number of times by Canadian trial courts — especially in drug cases involving "a tiny quantity of the proscribed drug" and theft cases where the "value of the stolen property is very low." Justice Arbour wrote:

Generally, the justifications for a *de minimis* excuse are: (1) it reserves the application of the criminal law to serious misconduct; (2) it protects an accused from the stigma of a criminal conviction and from the imposition of severe penalties for relatively trivial conduct; and (3) it saves courts from being swamped by an enormous number of trivial cases.... In part, the theory is based on a notion that the evil to be prevented by the offence section has not actually occurred. This is consistent with the dual fundamental principle of criminal justice that there is no culpability for harmless and blameless conduct....

The chief justice, speaking for the Court majority in the Foundation case, saw a role for the *de minimis* rule, although one that had its own problems of ambiguity. But it is one that does not infringe on the Court's basic holding. She stated:

Finally, Arbour J. argues that parents who face criminal charges as a result of corrective force will be able to rely on the defences of necessity and *de minimis*. The defence of necessity, I agree, is available, but only in situations where corrective force is not in issue, like saving a child from imminent danger. As for the defence of *de minimis*, it is equally or more vague and difficult in application than the reasonableness defence offered by section 43.

CRUEL AND UNUSUAL TREATMENT OR PUNISHMENT?

Question: Does section 43 of the Criminal Code offend section 12 of the Charter, which guarantees the "right not to be subject to any cruel and unusual treatment or punishment"? The Foundation argued that such a violation occurs whenever parents or teachers use physical force against children of whatever age.

Answer: None of the Court Justices saw any merit to the Foundation argument. Chief Justice McLachlin, speaking for the Court majority stated that section 12 of the Charter relates to action by the State.

- Parents, as such, are not agents of the State. Thus, any action on their part against children cannot be seen as action by the State. Section 12 of the Charter does not apply to the parents.
- Teachers, especially, those employed by government, may be seen as employees of the State. However, the chief justice stated that section 43, as it has been interpreted and limited by the Court, cannot rise to the level of cruel and unusual punishment.

The chief justice wrote:

> The conduct permitted by section 43 does not in any event rise to the level of being "cruel and unusual," or so excessive as to outrage standards of decency.... Section 43 permits only corrective force that is reasonable. Conduct cannot be at once both reasonable and an outrage to standards of decency. Corrective force that might rise to the level of "cruel and unusual" remains subject to criminal prosecution.

A POLL ON SPANKING

Quebecers are far less likely than other Canadians to spank or slap their children. This was a finding of a *Globe and Mail*/CTV poll of Canadian parents conducted by Ipsos-Reid and published in a *Globe and Mail* article by Erin Anderssen and Anne McIlroy titled "Quebec Distinct in Nursery Too, Poll Finds" (April 10, 2004).

Nationally, 42 percent of those polled agreed with the statement that they had spanked or slapped their children for disciplinary reasons. Regionally, the results were as follows:

British Columbia	52%
Alberta	60%
Saskatchewan/Manitoba	46%
Ontario	45%
Quebec	22%
Atlantic provinces	42%

The age of the children did not seem to be a factor. Results were consistent among parents of children under five, aged six to eleven, and those twelve and over.

Nationally, the survey found that 60 percent of Canadian parents agreed with the statement that politicians and the courts are too involved in making decisions about how they parent. Regionally, the results were as follows:

British Columbia	61%
Alberta	74%
Saskatchewan/Manitoba	84%
Ontario	61%
Quebec	51%
Atlantic provinces	48%

The survey also found that most Canadian parents seem satisfied with the job they are doing as parents. A strong majority said they were doing as well (50 percent) or better (43 percent) at raising their children than their own parents did. More than 60 percent said they are more permissive with their children than their parents were with them.

The poll is considered accurate to within 3.9 percentage points, nineteen times out of twenty, although the margin of error is larger in the regional results.

REFERENCES AND FURTHER READING
* Cited by the Supreme Court of Canada

Anderssen, Erin, and Anne McIlroy. 2004. "Quebec Distinct in Nursery Too, Poll Finds." *Globe and Mail*, April 10.

Bernard, Claire. 1998. *Corporal Punishment as a Means of Correcting Children*. Quebec: Commission des droits de la personne et des droits de la jeunesse.*

Canada. Department of Justice.1994. *Reforming the General Part of the Criminal Code: A Consultation Paper*. Ottawa.*

Canadian Bar Association. Criminal Recodification Task Force. 1992. *Principles of Criminal Liability: Proposals for a New General Part of the Criminal Code of Canada*. Ottawa.*

Canadian Committee on Corrections. 1969. *Report of the Canadian Committee on Corrections — Toward Unity: Criminal Justice and Corrections*. Ottawa: Queen's Printer.*

Committee on the Rights of the Child. 2003. Consideration of Reports Submitted by State Parties Under Article 40 of the Convention, Thirty-fourth Session, CRC/C/15/Add. 215.

Department of Justice. *Reforming the General Part of the Criminal Code: A Consultation Paper*. Ottawa, 1994.*

Edwards, Steven. 2003. "Slap Spankers with Criminal Code, UN Advises Canada." *National Post*, October 8.

Greene, Sharon D. 1998. "The Unconstitutionality of Section 43 of the Criminal Code: Children's Right to Be Protected from Physical Assault, Part 1." *Criminal Law Quarterly* 41, no. 3: 288–317.*

Law Reform Commission of Canada. 1984. *Working Paper 38, Assault.* Ottawa.*

McGillivray, Anne. 1997. "He'll Learn It on His Body: Disciplining Childhood in Canadian Law." *International Journal of Children's Rights* 5, no. 2: 193–242.*

Newell, Peter. 1989. *Children Are People Too: The Case Against Physical Punishment.* London: Bedford Square Press.*

Sharpe, Robert, Katherine E. Swinton, and Kent Roach. 2002. The Charter of Rights and Freedoms. 2nd ed. Toronto: Irwin Law.*

"Spanking Is Permitted, But Mind the New Rules." 2004. *Globe and Mail*, January 3.

Stuart, Don. 2001. *Canadian Criminal Law: A Treatise.* 4th ed. Scarborough, ON: Carswell.*

Vallis, Mary. 2003. "No Country in the World Has Criminalized Spanking." *National Post*, October 8.

Wente, Margaret. 2004. "Worse Things than Spanking." *Globe and Mail*, January 3.

CHAPTER 2

VIOLENT YOUNG OFFENDERS: SETTING AND APPLYING STANDARDS

There are two public policies concerning youth that may sometimes conflict: (1) acceptance of the young as vulnerable and (2) the need to protect the public from violent young offenders. The first policy focuses on rehabilitation of the young rather than imprisonment, favouring help rather than punishment and removal from society. The second policy centres on what is needed to protect society from the kind of behaviour seriously hurtful to others. In effect, society, as a matter of principle, would hold the young offender to the same general standard of responsibility as an adult.

In this chapter, the tension between these policies will be expressed in real-life scenarios involving violent young offenders whose victims are often other young people. We will see how Parliament has tried to set new approaches by marking certain crimes as more serious and thus, in Parliament's view, requiring greater youth explanation — or for the accused youth to face the prospect of treatment as an adult criminal.

Drawing the lines between youth and adult treatment is no easy legislative task. It requires words and concepts that may sound like legalisms, such as the term *presumptive offence*. But such words are intended to help judges, especially youth court judges, establish guides that might be followed by other judges nationally — and thus avoid judges making individual law that reflect their values and bias. Recall the youth court judge quoted by Justice Arbour in the spanking case, cited in the last chapter. That judge justified the spanking by saying it was no more that he (the judge) had experienced as a youth.

Among the issues discussed in this chapter are:

- What is a presumptive offence under the Youth Criminal Justice Act?
- What is the purpose of a youth sentence under the criminal law?
- Can young people be tried and sentenced as adults?
- Under the criminal law, does the Charter of Rights and Freedoms apply to young persons?
- What, if any, consent must police get before taking a statement from a young person charged with an offence?
- Are the numbers of violent young offenders on the increase?

In a general sense, the actions of "violent young offenders" could include any violent behaviour of the young. It might involve a young person who steals a car or drives it in a way that endangers the safety of others, including police officers in pursuit. Applying the criminal law to such behaviour is another matter.

The criminal law can involve penalties. For adults found guilty of a criminal offence, statute may compel a court to impose fines (the proceeds of which go to the State, not necessarily to the victim) or minimum terms of imprisonment. Such penalties are not primarily directed toward rehabilitation. During the time that someone is incarcerated, society is protected from that person repeating violent behaviour. But sitting in a jail cell may do little to reform the felon.

Imprisonment in a free society affects basic rights. The common law — that is, law made by judges — has long treated such government action with great scrutiny. The courts have strictly interpreted any action by government that would deny the liberty of a person. Indeed, much of the Charter of Rights and Freedoms is directed toward protecting the individual who comes into contact with the criminal justice system, such as the police or the courts.

Over the years, an even more protective shield has been cast over young persons who have been brought into contact with the criminal law. This shield is made up of the common law and of statute that has long deemed young people as vulnerable — not being able to fully understand the difference between right and wrong, and make judgments as would adults. If young people cannot differentiate between right and wrong, should they be held liable for violating any particular criminal law?

For many years, there has been a separate system for ensuring fairness to the young person brought into contact with the criminal law. That system ranges from the contact of police with the youth in questioning and making an arrest, to an informal court trial conducted by special judges. If found guilty, a youth may be given a lesser sentence than an adult, and in that regard, a sentence that favours rehabilitation over punishment.

Youth crime and society's perception of it have changed over the years. To some extent, that change, partly reflected in data and in dramatic incidents (some of which will be related), have influenced the enactment of new laws importantly including the Youth Criminal Justice Act (YCJA), Statutes of Canada 2002.

The YCJA, among other things, makes it possible for young persons (defined as between fourteen and eighteen) to be sentenced as adults for certain serious (and usually violent) crimes that the YCJA lists as presumptive offences. These include:

- first-degree or second-degree murder;
- attempt to commit murder;
- manslaughter;

- aggravated sexual assault; and
- "an offence in the commission of which a young person causes or attempts to cause serious bodily harm."

There is a significant difference between the length of imprisonment for an adult sentence, such as first-degree murder, and a youth sentence for the same crime. The YCJA leaves it to the youth court judge to decide whether a young person charged with a presumptive offence should be sentenced as an adult.

In this regard, the accused young person, under the YCJA, carries the burden of demonstrating to the youth court judge why an adult sentence should not be imposed. To do this, the young person must demonstrate that the youth sentence is of sufficient length to hold him/her accountable. Under the YCJA, the Crown does not have to show that the youth has lost entitlement to a youth sentence. In effect, the burden under the law shifts to the accused. This is called reverse onus.

These are among the issues raised by reverse onus and discussed in this chapter:

- Does switching the burden of proof, that is, reverse onus, violate section 7 of the Charter of Rights and Freedoms? Does it deny a young person's right not to be denied liberty "except in accordance with the principles of fundamental justice"?
- Can young people who commit more serious crimes be held to more serious penalties?
- May young persons subject to adult sentences also have their identities revealed?

A case that discusses and rules upon these issues is *The Queen v. D.B.*, decided in a 5-4 decision by the Supreme Court of Canada on May 16, 2008. Justice Rosalie Abella wrote the majority decision, and Justice Marshall Rothstein the dissent.

Note, however, the incident giving rise to the offence occurred in 2003. The decision of the Supreme Court of Canada was handed down more than four years later. The course of justice often is ponderous. But more to the point in dealing with young offenders, the accused often begins an encounter with the criminal justice system as a youth and the sentence is delivered when that individual is an adult.

THE QUEEN v. D.B.

At the time of the offence, D.B., the accused, was seventeen, a juvenile whose identity was protected under the Youth Criminal Justice Act (YCJA).

On December 13, 2003, D.B. went to a Hamilton, Ontario, shopping mall with some friends. Insults were exchanged with another group of young men, and two of them began to fight. Then D.B. turned to eighteen-year-old Jonathan Romero and said, "Me and you are going to fight right now." Romero answered, "No."

Romero's arms were down at his sides when D.B. punched him on the right side of his neck and face. The punch was described as a "sucker punch." Romero was neither prepared nor ready for it.

Romero fell to the ground from the force of the punch. D.B. did not let up. He jumped on top of Romero and hit him four times on the face and neck. Romero, having been knocked unconscious, was unable to defend himself. At that point, D.B. got up and fled back to the shopping mall.

Two of the other youths who had been fighting then stopped and, with three employees from a nearby store, tried to help Romero. An ambulance was called. When it arrived, Romero had no vital signs. He later died of his injuries.

Inside the mall, D.B. was heard to say, "You missed it. It was one punch. The guy's not even fuckin' moving." He changed his clothes in a nearby restaurant and stowed the old clothes in a knapsack that he gave to someone else. He then went to a friend's home, talking about the fight on the way. Later that evening, he went to a nightclub. He left with friends around closing time.

In the taxi, D.B. learned via a cell phone call that Romero had died. He stayed that night at a friend's house. The next morning, police arrived at the friend's home. D.B. attempted to flee out the back door but was caught and arrested.

D.B. pleaded guilty to manslaughter. He asked the trial judge for a youth sentence rather than that of an adult. The Crown opposed this request. However, the trial judge rejected the Crown's request and imposed a youth sentence on D.B.

In an unreported decision, the trial judge stated:

> You [D.B.] are to be the subject of an intensive rehabilitative custody and supervision order for a period of three years, and committed into a continuous period of intensive rehabilitative custody for a period of thirty months and serve the remainder of the sentence under conditional supervision in the community in accordance with section 105 of the *Youth Criminal Justice Act*.
>
> In my view the maximum period of a youth sentence is necessary to achieve the desired ends of the rehabilitation programme, and for that reason I have not given credit for the one year period of pre-trial custody.

The trial court was aware of D.B.'s record through a predisposition assessment when it imposed the maximum period of a youth sentence. D.B. had frequently been involved in physical fights with his peers. And he had been suspended from school,

> numerous times primarily for disruptive behaviour, verbal aggression, and disrespectful and intimidating conduct towards school staff. At

the time of the offence, D.B. was bound by two separate probation orders arising out of prior convictions for possession of stolen property and robbery. Both offences involved threats and intimidation. While he was in custody awaiting disposition and sentence for manslaughter, D.B. was involved in several assaultive incidents with other inmates and staff members.

REHABILITATION VERSUS INCARCERATION

The trial court judge found there was a basis for rehabilitation, which was a more desired alternative to incarceration. The trial judge stated that D.B.'s offence had to be considered "most serious" and that the act was "stupid, impulsive … borne of exuberance of youth and a misguided need for image before the offender's peers" leading to a "tragic outcome."

In response to the Crown's concerns about D.B.'s maturity, character, background, and previous record, the trial judge felt that the intensive rehabilitative custody and supervision order provisions of the YCJA could address such areas. The trial judge concluded that "the need for rehabilitation of this offender and … the protection of society are better achieved through the intensive rehabilitation programme available through a youth sentence than through a more protracted period of incarceration which may result from the imposition of an adult sentence."

Justice Abella, speaking for the majority in *The Queen v. D.B.*, agreed. She stated:

> There is no doubt that D.B. committed a serious offence with tragic consequences. It remains to determine whether the maximum allowable youth sentence he received from the trial judge should be set aside.

The purpose of sentencing under the YCJA is expressed as follows in section 38(1): "The purpose of sentencing under section 42 (youth sentences) is to hold a young person accountable for an offence through the imposition of just sanctions that have meaningful consequences for the young person and that promote his or her rehabilitation and reintegration into society, thereby contributing to the long-term protection of the public."

D.B. had been previously convicted for possession of stolen property and robbery, both involving threats and intimidation, and was bound by two separate probation orders at the time of the offence. He had a history of mental health issues and behavioural problems in school.

He expressed remorse for his offence prior to sentencing and had made some positive steps while in pre-trial detention. The predisposition assessment recommended that he be treated in a therapeutic milieu, including a highly structured environment with integrated academic and social programming, and also concluded that societal as well as his personal needs could best be met by keeping D.B. in the juvenile justice correctional system rather than exposing him to more hardened criminals.

Justice Abella recited the detailed order of the trial judge set out above and concluded:

Section 72(1) of the YCJA sets out a number of matters to be considered by the youth justice court in reaching its opinion about whether a youth sentence would be sufficient. The reasons for the sentence of the trial judge reflect that he did so. His weighing of these matters to reach his opinion about sufficiency is a task that must attract deference in this court. The Crown does not suggest that he acted on an improper principle or considered extraneous matters. It essentially argues that he did the weighing wrongly. In my view, that is not enough to warrant the setting aside of his decision.

It was not a question of the trial court applying an incorrect principle of law or considering improper evidence. In that regard, Justice Abella noted that the trial judge had observed the witnesses and their demeanour, and had heard their testimony. The appellate court could look at the written record and ask whether there had been an error of law.

The major part of the decision of the Supreme Court of Canada in *The Queen v. D.B.* centres on the role of the Charter on the YCJA.

YOUTH OR ADULT SENTENCE: THE CHARTER

As was noted before, the YCJA places the burden on the youth convicted of a presumptive offence — such as, in this matter, manslaughter — to justify why a youth sentence rather than an adult sentence should be imposed. Under the YCJA, the failure on the part of the convicted youth to carry this burden *requires* the trial judge to sentence that person as an adult. The judge is denied choice in the matter. This is how the Supreme Court of Canada summarized the relevant provision of the YCJA:

A young person may, however, under section 63(1) of the Act, "make an application for an order that he or she is not liable to an adult sentence." The court is then required to consider the factors set out in section 72(1), namely: "the seriousness and circumstances of the offence, and the age, maturity, character, background and previous record of the young person and any other factors that the court considers relevant."

The onus of satisfying the court about these matters is on the young person (section 72(2)). *Consequently, if the young person is unable to persuade the court that a youth sentence "would have sufficient length to hold the young person accountable for his or her offending behaviour," an adult sentence shall be imposed*[emphasis added] (section 72(1)(b)). The default position, in other words, is an adult sentence.

Even the most severe youth sentence, according to the trial judge in the case of D.B., involves far less incarceration time than an adult sentence for the crime. Further, the youth sentence is directed toward rehabilitation, not punishment or protecting the public from a potentially violent offender by incarceration.

Counsel for D.B. argued that the presumptive provision of the YCJA was invalid because it violated section 7 of the Charter of Rights and Freedoms, which, as we stated before, is part of the Constitution of Canada. If a statute conflicts with the Charter, then to the extent of the conflict, the Charter sets the standard. This means that in any conflict with the Charter, either all or part of the statute will be set aside to the extent of that conflict. Both the trial court and the appellate court agreed with counsel for D.B. It was in such a context that the matter came before the Supreme Court of Canada.

THE SUPREME COURT OF CANADA DECIDES:
THE MAJORITY OPINION

In this 5-4 decision, Justice Abella spoke for the Court majority. The Court first asked whether the presumptive provision of the YCJA was valid as measured by section 7 of the Charter, which provides, "Everyone has the right to life, liberty and security of the person and the right not to be deprived thereof except in accordance with the principles of fundamental justice."

The analysis of section 7 comes in two parts, Justice Abella said. First, was there a denial of life, liberty, or security of the person? And, second, if so, was that denial in accord with the principles of fundamental justice?

As to the first part of the analysis, there was no question and no objection stated by the Crown: the "reverse burden of proof" raises the possibility of imprisonment or the threat of imprisonment.

It was the second part of section 7 that required further discussion by Justice Abella: Did the reverse onus rule of the YCJA affect a principle of fundamental justice? Yes, said Justice Abella. Without a finding that the young are vulnerable, that they have a reduced capacity for moral judgment, and that this vulnerability constituted a principle of fundamental justice, section 7 of the Charter simply would not apply. Putting it differently, section 7 of the Charter can only apply if it affects a principle of fundamental justice.

The Court found that principle by looking at a number of sources. First, it looked to the YCJA itself. In section 3(1)(b), the YCJA makes clear what the courts have long recognized: "The criminal justice system for young persons must be separate from that of adults." But why must there be this separation? Justice Abella stated:

> Because of their age, young people have heightened vulnerability, less maturity and a reduced

capacity for moral judgment. This entitles them to a presumption of diminished moral blameworthiness or culpability. This presumption is the principle at issue here and it is a presumption that has resulted in the entire youth sentencing scheme, with its unique approach to punishment.

For example, Justice Abella wrote, there are numerous sentencing provisions in the YCJA to protect, presumptively, young persons from custody. Confronted with a crime committed by a young person, police must consider whether alternatives outside the court exist. Section 4 of the YCJA declares that such measures are "presumed to be adequate to hold a young person accountable ... if the young person has committed a non-violent offence and has not previously been found guilty of an offence."

Sections 38 and 39 of the YCJA also limit when a court may order custody. Before sentencing a young person to custody, the court must:

- believe that no reasonable alternative or combination of alternatives exists (section 39(2));
- know that the previous use of a non-custodial sentence does not preclude another non-custodial sentence (section 39(4));
- recognize that custody must not be a substitute for appropriate child protection, mental health, or other social measures (section 39(5));
- consider a pre-sentence report and any sentencing proposal made by the young person or the counsel present (section 39(6));
- state reasons why a non-custodial sentence is inadequate (section 39(9));
- consider all available sanctions other than custody first (section 38(2)(d)); and

- ensure that the sentence is the least restrictive one capable of holding the young person accountable, bearing in mind the nature of the offence (section 38(2)(e)).

These provisions are core goals of the YCJA. But, it was not enough for Justice Abella to conclude that they reflected a principle of fundamental justice, namely that the young have heightened vulnerability and a reduced capacity for moral blameworthiness. She next looked to the history of the criminal law relating to the young. She referred to the English common law, academic writings, and the many laws controlling youth crime in Canada, dating from 1857. There she found an ongoing legislative recognition of diminished criminal responsibility on the part of young offenders. "Canada," she said, "has consistently acknowledged the diminished responsibility and distinctive vulnerability of young persons in all of the YCJA's statutory predecessors." (See, "Challenge Question: A Matter of Principle.")

Indeed, Justice Abella found additional support for the vulnerability of the child as a legal principle in international law. The preamble to the YCJA notes this point in its preamble. Canada became a signing party to the United Nations Convention on the Rights of the Child in 1992. Section 1 of that convention states:

[Those signing the convention] recognize the right of every child alleged as, accused of, or recognized as having infringed the penal law to be treated in a manner consistent with the promotion of the child's sense of dignity and worth, which reinforces the child's respect for the human rights and fundamental freedoms of others and which takes into account the child's age and the desirability of promoting the child's reintegration and the child's assuming a constructive role in society.

That legal principle translated into a principle of fundamental justice, according to Justice Abella. She quoted from and relied upon past Supreme Court of Canada decisions as well as academic writings. For example, she noted the decision of former Chief Justice Antonio Lamer of the Supreme Court of Canada in *Reference re Young Offenders Act (P.E.I.)*, [1991] 1 *Supreme Court of Canada Reports* 252, at p. 268, who said of the then controlling juvenile justice law, "What distinguishes this legislation from the Criminal Code is the fact that it creates a special regime for young persons. The essence of the young offenders legislation is a distinction based on age and on the diminished responsibility associated with this distinction."

The result of this review of past Canadian legislation and the laws of other western nations led Justice Abella, speaking for the Court majority in *The Queen v. D.B.*, to say that "a broad consensus reflecting society's values and interests exists…. The principle of a presumption of diminished moral culpability in young persons is fundamental to our notions of how a fair legal system ought to operate." And, Justice Abella added, this principle of fundamental justice is one that the courts can administer. It is manageable.

APPLYING THE PRINCIPLE OF FUNDAMENTAL JUSTICE TO "REVERSE ONUS"

Is the onus provision consistent with the principle of fundamental justice that young people are entitled to a presumption of diminished moral responsibility? As noted, ordinarily the Crown can seek an adult sentence for a young person over the age of fourteen who has been found guilty of certain indictable offences.

The young person must be notified of the Crown's intention and, once notified, can elect to be tried by a youth court judge or, in the Ontario Superior Court of Justice, by a judge alone or with a jury following a preliminary inquiry. The onus is on the Crown.

If the Crown does not persuade the court, a youth sentence will be imposed.

Again, as noted, under the YCJA, the young person charged with or found guilty of a presumptive offence, however, must apply for an order that he or she is not liable to an adult sentence so that a youth sentence can be imposed (section 63(1)). In making its decision, the court must consider whether a youth sentence "would have sufficient length to hold the young person accountable for his or her offending behaviour" (sections 72(1)(a) and (1)(b)). In deciding whether it would be a sufficiently long sentence, the court is to consider "the seriousness and circumstances of the offence, and the age, maturity, character, background and previous record of the young person and any other factors that the court considers relevant (section 72(1))."

Justice Abella probed the effect of a presumptive sentence on a young person. She wrote:

> In the case of presumptive offences, it is the young person who must satisfy the court of the factors justifying a youth sentence, whereas it is normally the Crown who is required to satisfy the court of any factors justifying a more severe sentence. A maximum adult sentence in the case of presumptive offences is, by definition, more severe than the maximum permitted for a youth sentence. A youth sentence for murder cannot exceed ten years; for second-degree murder, seven; and for manslaughter, three. The maximum adult sentence for these offences is life in prison.
>
> A young person should receive, at the very least, the same procedural benefit afforded to a convicted adult on sentencing, namely, that the burden is on the Crown to demonstrate why a more severe sentence is necessary and appropriate in any given case. The onus on the young person

reverses this traditional onus on the Crown and is, consequently, a breach of section 7 [of the Charter].

EFFECT OF REVERSE ONUS

Justice Abella, in *The Queen v. D.B.*, stated that an adult sentence can be imposed on a youth. But that sentence must be justified by the seriousness of the offence and the circumstances of the offender.

This means, Justice Abella said,

> [that the Crown is obliged to prove, beyond a reasonable doubt, any aggravating factors in sentencing on which it relies. Putting the onus on the young person to prove the *absence* of aggravating factors in order to justify a youth sentence, rather than on the Crown to prove the aggravating factors that justify a lengthier adult sentence, reverses the onus.
>
> In my view, both the informality of the sentencing procedure as to the admissibility of evidence and the wide discretion given to the trial judge in imposing sentence are factors militating *in favour of* the retention of the criminal standard of proof beyond a reasonable doubt at sentencing.
>
> Because the sentencing process poses the ultimate jeopardy to an individual enmeshed in the criminal process, it is just and reasonable that he be granted the protection of the reasonable doubt rule at this vital juncture of the process.... It is clear law that where the Crown advances aggravating facts in sentencing which are contested, the Crown must establish those facts beyond reasonable doubt.

YOU BE THE JUDGE

A MATTER OF DEFENCE: PUBLIC PROTECTION

THE FACTS

D.B.'s record both before and after he struck and killed his victim in a shopping mall fight was serious and lengthy. He had been involved in two parole violations following the fight that led to his second-degree murder conviction. As well, he had been involved in fights with other youths while incarcerated.

The Crown prosecutor argued that, on the face of that record, it should not have to bear the burden of proving D.B. should be sentenced as an adult offender and that the publication ban masking his identity should be removed. D.B., the Crown seemed to say, was a threat to society.

In its argument to the Supreme Court of Canada, the Crown seemed to have set out its argument in the alternative. That is, assume the burden of proof in terms of presumed offences under the YCJA was overturned because of section 7 of the Charter as a violation of liberty not "in accordance with the principles of fundamental justice."

Still, the Crown stated, the "sentencing provisions [of the YCJA] served the goals of accountability, protection of the public, and public confidence in the administration of justice." As such, they should be sustained.

THE ISSUE

Who should have the burden of proving if D.B. should be sentenced as an adult?

POINTS TO CONSIDER

- For our purposes, assume, as indeed was the case, that the Court had ruled the presumed offences under the YCJA in terms of burden of proof were a violation of section 7 of the Charter.
- The question now is whether the Charter contains another provision that would otherwise support the Crown's position.
- In this regard, the Crown turned to section 1 of the Charter, which provides: "The Canadian Charter of Rights and Freedoms guarantees the rights and freedoms set out in it subject only to such reasonable limits prescribed by law as can be demonstrably justified in a free and democratic society."
- In effect, section 1 of the Charter would allow a section 7 infringement if it were a reasonable limit set out by law as can be justified in a free and democratic society.
- To meet the section 1 defence, two conditions must be met: (1) there must be a reasonable (rational) connection between the limitation on the liberty interest protected by section 7 of the Charter and the goal to be achieved — protection of the public; and (2) the limitation must be the minimum necessary to achieve the stated goal.

DISCUSSION

Justice Abella, speaking for the Supreme Court of Canada majority in *The Queen v. D.B.*, rejected the section 1

Charter defence raised by the Crown. She accepted that Parliament's objectives of accountability, public safety, and public confidence indeed were proper. But, she insisted that individual Charter rights could be safeguarded while at the same time rights set out by Parliament were protected. Thus, the need continued for the Crown to carry the burden of proof in demonstrating the need for an adult sentence.

THE YOUNG OFFENDER: STILL ACCOUNTABLE
The young offender still remains accountable. Justice Abella stated:

> This does not make young persons less accountable for serious offences; it makes them *differently* accountable. Nor does it mean that a court cannot impose an adult sentence on a young person. It means that before a court can do so, the Crown, not the young person, should have the burden of showing that the presumption of diminished moral culpability has been rebutted and that the young person is no longer entitled to its protection.
>
> Promoting the protection of the public is equally well served by putting this onus on the Crown, where it belongs. The Crown may still persuade a youth court judge that an adult sentence or the lifting of a publication ban is warranted where a serious crime has been committed. And young persons will continue to be accountable

in accordance with their personal circumstances and the seriousness of the offence.
But the burden of demonstrating that more
serious consequences are warranted will be,
as it properly is for adults, on the Crown.

YOU BE THE JUDGE

THE QUEEN V. D.B. — PUBLICATION BAN

THE FACTS

D.B. was given a youth sentence. As part of this youth sentence, the YCJA provides for a publication ban, which prohibits any publication of the accused youth's identity. That is
why D.B. is referred to by initials rather than by his full and
legal name. However, the burden of showing that the ban
should remain is placed on the young offender.

THE ISSUES

Who has the burden of showing why a publication ban
should be removed? What must be proved to meet that
burden?

POINTS TO CONSIDER

- The publication ban is only technically part
  of the YCJA sentence. The reason for this is to

allow an appeal of any court order permitting the youth's identification.

- The YCJA imposes on the youth a "reverse onus" burden even if the court imposes a youth sentence. That is, the youth must show entitlement to a publication ban.
- The Crown prosecutor argued in *The Queen v. D.B.* that D.B. had the burden of showing why the publication ban should not be removed.
- In section 3(1)(b)(iii) of the YCJA, the young person's "enhanced procedural protection ... including their right to privacy" is stated to be a principle to be emphasized in the application of the Act.
- The *United Nations Standard Minimum Rules for the Administration of Juvenile Justice* provides that "the juvenile's right to privacy shall be respected at all stages in order to avoid harm being caused to her or him by undue publicity or by the process of labelling" and declares that "in principle, no information that may lead to the identification of a juvenile offender shall be published."

DISCUSSION

Justice Abella, speaking for the Court majority in *The Queen v. D.B.*, ruled that the Crown had the burden of showing why the publication ban should be removed. She linked this conclusion to the sentence's effect on a young offender. As such, her reasoning relating to section 7 of the Charter applied. She wrote:

I see the onus on young persons to demonstrate why they remain entitled to the ongoing protection of a publication ban to be a violation of section 7. As discussed, the effect of the reverse onus provisions is that if a young person is unable to persuade the court that a youth sentence should be imposed, an adult sentence is imposed.

When an adult sentence is imposed, the young person loses the protection of a publication ban. But even if the young person succeeds in discharging the reverse onus and receives a youth sentence, the YCJA imposes an additional onus by requiring the young person to apply for the ban that normally accompanies a youth sentence.

In s. 3(1)(b)(iii) of the YCJA ... the young person's "enhanced procedural protection ... *including their right to privacy*," is stipulated to be a principle to be emphasized in the application of the Act.

Scholars agree that "publication increases a youth's self-perception as an offender, disrupts the family's abilities to provide support, and negatively affects interaction with peers, teachers, and the surrounding community" (Nicholas Bala, *Young Offenders Law* (1997), at p. 215). Professor Doob ... testified about this issue before the Standing Committee on Justice: "I think you'd be hard-pressed to find a single professional who has worked in this area who would be in favour of the publication of names. From the very beginning when this was proposed in May 1998, I'd never heard anybody give a single reasoned, principled argument for doing it. Now, there are some other arguments for doing it having to do essentially with vindictiveness, but in terms of actually trying to be constructive in any way, as I said, I would certainly find it very difficult to find anybody who has done any research on this kind of issue who would support it. It just seems to me to be a gratuitous meanness."

International instruments have also recognized the negative impact of such media attention on young people. The *United Nations Standard Minimum Rules for the Administration of Juvenile Justice* ("Beijing Rules," adopted by General Assembly Resolution A/RES/40/33 on November 29, 1985) provide in rule 8 ("Protection of privacy") that "the juvenile's right to privacy shall be respected at all stages in order to avoid harm being caused to her or him by undue publicity or by the process of labelling" and declare that "in principle, no information that may lead to the identification of a juvenile offender shall be published."

The foregoing demonstrates that lifting a ban on publication makes the young person vulnerable to greater psychological and social stress. Accordingly, it renders the sentence significantly more severe. A publication ban is part of a young person's sentence (section 75(4)). It is therefore subject to the same presumption as the rest of his or her sentence. Losing the protection of a publication ban renders the sentence more severe. The onus should therefore be, as with the imposition of an adult sentence, on the Crown to justify the enhanced severity, rather than on the youth to justify retaining the protection to which he or she is otherwise presumed to be entitled. The reversal of this onus too is a breach of section 7.

DISSENTING OPINION

Justice Rothstein and three other justices dissented from the majority in *The Queen v. D.B.*

First, Justice Rothstein argued that the only purpose of the appeal provisions of the YCJA relating to publication bans was to give a limited right to seek court review where one would not otherwise exist. The reality, he said, is that publication bans simply are not part of any sentence. Publishing a story about the alleged crime does not, as such, impose any kind of sentence on the defendant, though it surely may be argued that such publication may hold the defendant up to ridicule.

Further, he argued that the provision of the YCJA relating to the presumption of publication bans does not involve issues involving section 7 of the Charter. He stated:

The liberty interest protected by section 7 encompasses freedom from physical restraint and protection of an individual's personal autonomy.... Since the presumption of publication does not cause physical restraint on young offenders nor does it prevent them from making fundamental personal choices, the interests sought to be protected in this case do not fall within the liberty interest protected by section 7....

Where, as here, the security right in section 7 is being invoked on the basis of an impact on the individual's psychological security, "serious state-imposed psychological stress" must be demonstrated: *The Queen v. Morgentaler*, [1988] 1 *Supreme Court of Canada Reports* 30.... The two factors which must be evaluated [are]: the psychological harm must be state imposed, meaning that the harm must result from the actions of the state, and the psychological prejudice must be serious.

I accept that publication of a young offender's identity may increase a youth's self-perception as an offender, disrupt the ability of a youth's family to provide support, and negatively affect interaction with peers, teachers, and the surrounding community.... However, the difficulty in this case is not the *existence of harm* but rather whether that harm is *state induced*. In my view, it is not.

As Bastarache J. [for the Supreme Court of Canada in another matter] emphasized ... it is "inappropriate to hold government accountable for harms that are brought about by third parties who are not in any sense acting as agents of the state." He explicitly stated that psychological stress resulting from media coverage can only underlie a section 7 claim *where it can be directly linked to state action*.

In [this] case, there is *no* state action: the stigma and labelling that may arise from release of the young offender's identity result from the actions of the media and broader society. The harm is a product of media coverage and society's reaction to young offenders and to the crimes they commit.

Although Parliament has recognized that unwanted publicity and the public's negative reaction may harm young offenders convicted of crimes, and has afforded the vast majority of them a degree of protection by requiring a publication ban (section 110(1) YCJA), this does not mean that the state is responsible for *imposing* the harm that may result without the publication ban.

AGE COUNTS UNDER THE YCJA:
OTHER JURISDICTIONS

In Canada, only young offenders aged fourteen and older, but less than eighteen, charged with committing a "presumed" offence, may be sentenced as an adult. It is here where the reverse onus, earlier described, comes into play. Other countries, on the matter of sentencing young people as adults, have taken positions similar to that of Canada. The matter of reverse onus, however, is another matter.

FRANCE, THE EUROPEAN UNION, AND THE UNITED KINGDOM

A government-sponsored study in France recently recommended that judges be permitted to sentence youths as young as age twelve to detention for crime. The French minister of justice had called for an overhaul of the juvenile justice system saying that it was not equipped to deal with younger and more violent criminals.

If the proposal were adopted, it would reduce the age for such sentencing from thirteen. And, as such, it would be in line with many other countries in the European Union and the United Kingdom.

The French proposal coincided with a suggestion from a spokesperson for the French president who said that toddlers could be screened for "violent tendencies" to identify those who might commit crimes in the future. The suggestion had been made in 2008 by the French president himself and a major French public health research institute. At the time, opponents of the proposal mustered fifty thousand signatures in opposition (Sachs 2008).

THE MEDIA'S RESPONSE

The following editorial on *The Queen v. D.B.* appeared in the *Globe and Mail* on May 17, 2008:

Seldom in recent years has a constitutional decision seemed so conjured out of thin air. Yesterday the Supreme Court of Canada struck down the youth-justice law's presumption that 14- to 17-year-olds who commit the most serious offences, such as murder, will receive adult penalties. Its legal justification was simply baffling. It can be understood only as a policy choice, usurping Parliament's role.

On what constitutional grounds did the court decide the presumption cannot stand? Madam Justice Rosalie Abella, writing for the 5-4 majority, said it violates a "principle of fundamental justice" — a value so basic to Canadians that the legal system would fall into disrepute without it. The principle is that young people in general should be held less culpable for their crimes than adults. On that, Judge Abella was right — but the law already embodies that principle.

The Youth Criminal Justice Act is a delicate political compromise and a balancing of competing societal interests. The act's main thrust is overwhelmingly liberal: that young people should be kept out of jail if at all possible, especially if their crimes are non-violent (arson is considered a non-violent crime, as is leading police on a 160-km-an-hour car chase). The government argued that the act took into account public safety by presuming that the few youths who commit the most serious crimes (murder, attempted murder, manslaughter, aggravated assault or three serious violent offences) would receive adult penalties. (The presumption covered those 16 and 17 in 1995, and was extended to 14-and-15-year-olds in 2003.)

That presumption can be overcome, however, by the convicted youth. And the judge is required to invite the youth to argue against the presumption. And any arguments the youth and his lawyer make are presented in the context of the youth-crime law, which stresses the importance of rehabilitation. And even some of the adult penalties have been modified for youths. For instance, a first-degree murder conviction for adults brings an automatic life sentence with no parole eligibility for 25 years. A first-degree murder conviction for 16- and 17-year-olds also brings life, but parole eligibility is set at 10 years; for 14-and 15-year-olds, it's set at seven years. The law already establishes a separate criminal law for youth based on their lesser maturity.

As Mr. Justice Marshall Rothstein said for the minority, "The presumptive offence scheme *significantly* recognizes the age, reduced maturity and increased vulnerability of young persons." (His emphasis.) It cannot then violate Canadian notions of fundamental justice.

The [Supreme] Court has confused a legitimate policy choice with a fundamental value. In the United States, more than 2,000 juveniles convicted of murder are serving life sentences without a chance at parole. That would violate core Canadian principles — even for adults. Roughly a quarter of those 2,000-plus juveniles did not commit the murder themselves but were along on a robbery or other crime that turned deadly. That would shock Canadians' consciences. Nothing in Canadian law comes close. The youth-justice law as it stood did not offend basic values. This was a case of a court imposing its political viewpoint on the country with a constitutional sleight-of-hand. ("Sleight-of-Hand at the Supreme Court," 2008)

GUILT AND SENTENCING FOR MURDER UNDER THE YCJA

MEDICINE HAT KILLINGS

A fourteen-year-old Alberta girl was convicted in November 2007 of the first-degree murders of her mother, father, and eight-year-old brother. The killings took place in 2006 when the girl, who cannot be named under the YCJA, was twelve years old. Records indicate that she is Canada's youngest convicted killer.

The murders were carried out with her "boyfriend," Jeremy Steinke, then twenty-three. Steinke was tried before a jury. He steadfastly said that the murder of the eight-year-old was committed by his then twelve-year-old girlfriend. The jury deliberated for eleven hours before returning a verdict of guilty of murder in the first-degree in connection with the deaths of the three family members.

At the girl's trial, the Crown said that the pre-sentence report suggested that she had an "oppositional defiance disorder and conduct disorder." The Crown prosecutor, Stephanie Cleary, said of the fourteen-year-old: "The young person does not recognize that she has committed a crime, nor does she have any insight into her condition."

Justice Scott Brooker described the murders as "horrific." He said that the killing of the eight-year-old was "incomprehensible." He described the girl's mother and father as "wonderful parents" who loved their daughter and had tried to get her into family counselling.

Justice Brooker imposed a sentence known as intensive rehabilitative custody and supervision. This is a sentence rarely used under the YCJA — one for which young offenders must be diagnosed with some form of emotional or mental disorder. The girl will serve the maximum sentence of ten years, with credit for the eighteen months already spent in custody. Under the sentence, the first four years would be spent in a psychiatric hospital rather than a youth detention centre.

For Steinke, there is an automatic life sentence for a first-degree murder conviction. As well, there can be no eligibility for parole for twenty-five years ("Teen Gets Maximum Sentence for Medicine Hat Killings" 2007; "Steinke Found Guilty of First-Degree Murder" 2008).

REGINA TEEN SENTENCED AS AN ADULT

Larry Moser tried to help a Regina convenience store clerk who was fighting with a group of teens outside the store over a bag of sunflower seeds on Boxing Day, 2006. A sixteen-year-old, who cannot be named because of the YCJA, took part in the fight. He had a knife and stabbed Moser with it. Moser died from the wound.

The youth was tried and convicted of second-degree murder on November 28, 2008. The judge ordered the youth to serve a life sentence within the meaning of the YCJA. Practically, this means that the youth may not be considered for parole for seven years. The judge said the youth exhibited anti-social criminal behaviour and only the sentence imposed with its state-control would protect the public. At the time of trial and sentencing, the youth was eighteen ("Regina Teen Sentenced as Adult in Good Samaritan Killing" 2008).

GUNFIGHT IN TORONTO

Jane Creba, age fifteen, was shot to death on December 26, 2005. She was an innocent bystander, part of a crowd of Boxing Day shoppers in downtown Toronto. She was the victim of a gunfight between two groups, consisting in part of youths. The stray bullet that caused her death struck her in the back. Four men and two women were wounded in the crossfire.

Two youths and seven adult suspects were arrested, including J.S.R., who was seventeen at the time of the shooting. (J.S.R. was then six weeks from his eighteenth birthday — and, thus, nearly an adult. By the conclusion of trial and before sentencing, he was twenty-one.) At the scene of the gunfight, police found seven shell casings fired from the gun that killed Creba. J.S.R. was not charged with firing the pistol that killed Creba, but he was part of the gangs in conflict.

J.S.R. was arrested only forty minutes after the shooting. Police found a pistol in his possession that had been discharged and was later found responsible for wounding two bystanders (though not Creba). J.S.R., from the time of his arrest, said that the weapon police found had been handed to him after the shooting by the actual gunman, who J.S.R. named. It appeared that J.S.R. had been "cooperative" in the police investigation.

J.S.R. was the first of the nine arrested to go to trial. On December 7, 2008, the jury returned verdicts of guilty of second-degree murder in the death of Creba, as well as five weapons charges and two of six counts of aggravated assault. The courtroom was silent when the jury foreperson rose to announce the verdict. J.S.R. showed no emotion, other than his eyes initially fluttering. The trials of the remaining defendants were to take place later.

On December 11, 2008, the Crown stated that it wanted an adult sentence for J.S.R. If he were sentenced as an adult, he would be given life in prison with no eligibility for parole for seven years for the second-degree murder conviction. If J.S.R. were sentenced as a youth, he would receive a sentence of seven years, no more than four of which would normally be served in custody.

In the course of J.S.R.'s trial, the judge reduced the charge from second-degree murder to manslaughter. However, on appeal to the Ontario Court of Appeal, the more serious charge was reinstated. The appellate court ruled that a jury could find that J.S.R. could have participated in a "frenzied shootout." He could have "substantially contributed" to Creba's death by engaging in a gunfight. The reasoning seemed to be that if J.S.R. had not fired the gun, then the gun that had been fired and killed Creba likely would not have been fired.

Shortly before the gunfight, video cameras spotted J.S.R. as part of an aggressive group of young men moving about the Eaton Centre in downtown Toronto, close to where the gunfight took place. They had already "committed at least two ... crimes of violence in full public view." The attacks were edited out of the tapes shown to the jurors in the J.S.R. trial. J.S.R. already had been subject to a court order prohibiting him from even being on Yonge Street — the street, as it turned out, on which Creba had been shot.

J.S.R.'s sentencing was handed down by Ontario Justice Ian Nordheimer on April 24, 2009. J.S.R. was then twenty-one. It took Justice Nordheimer about an hour to read his sentencing judgment. Within the framework of the YCJA, Justice Nordheimer sentenced J.S.R. as an adult. In doing this, the judge stripped away J.S.R.'s anonymity. His identity was revealed to the public: Jorell Simpson-Rowe. His record of conviction was archived as open to the public.

While the YCJA rules out "denunciation" as an element of sentencing a youth, Justice Nordheimer said meaningful penalties are necessary in "society's interests." He noted what pre-sentence reports referred to as Simpson-Rowe's hellish upbringing. Still, said the judge, Simpson-Rowe was capable of distinguishing right from wrong. The judge said:

> In essence, as found by the jury, Mr. Simpson-Rowe opened fire with a semi-automatic pistol handgun on a crowded downtown street full of innocent citizens who were simply enjoying one of the rituals of the holiday season — Boxing Day sales.

The residents of this city are entitled to expect, indeed, they are entitled to insist, that they be able to go about such ordinary activities in relative safety and not be faced with the type of inexcusable violence that was unleashed by Mr. Simpson-Rowe and his associates.

The effect of Justice Nordheimer's sentence on Simpson-Rowe is that he will serve another three years and eight months in prison. He will be twenty-four when eligible for parole. (This may not be the end of the story. Lawyers for Simpson-Rowe announced that they will appeal the verdict — a matter that may take more than a few years.) (Appleby 2009b; Blatchford 2008; "Crown Seeks Adult Penalty in Creba Case" 2008; DiManno 2009; "Man, 20, Guilty of 2nd-Degree Murder in Jane Creba Shooting" 2008.)

CHALLENGE QUESTION

WHAT DO CURRENT STATISTICS PROVE?

Q: On the same day as the Supreme Court of Canada handed down its decision in The Queen v. D.B., Statistics Canada issued a report on youth crime in 2006. The report stated that youth crime in homicides had reached a historic high of fifty-four, an increase of 3 percent over 2005. Aside from an increase in youth homicides, what, if anything, is reflected in the quoted statistic? Does it indicate an increased level of crimes of violence by the young?

This question was suggested in a *Globe and Mail* article by Timothy Appleby (Appleby 2008a). He briefly cited the

Court's holding in *The Queen v. D.B.*, then reported the statistic quoted above.

Appleby asked for, received, and set out the following comments from experts — both police officers and youth advocates.

- Constable Scott Mills, Toronto's Crime Stoppers officer for schools, stated, "I deal with kids every day and they have told me personally, directly, many times: 'I'll [commit the crime] because the consequences are minimal....' So there has to be a deterrent, and as a street cop I can tell you this: I don't think the legislators or the judges were expecting fourteen- and fifteen-year-olds to be doing armed robberies and murders on the level they are today."

- Bernard Richard, a New Brunswick provincial advocate for children and youth, stated, "The research [of Statistics Canada and that which the Supreme Court cited in *The Queen v. D.B.*] is pretty solid — that as much as possible we should divert youth away from custodial sentences.... In the five years since the YCJA replaced the Young Offenders Act, the number of juveniles behind bars has dropped by a third."

The Statistics Canada report was taken from nationwide police reports. The data showed that youth crime was down 6 percent from a decade earlier, and down 25 percent from a 1991 peak. The youth crime rate was 6,885 for every 100,000 young people. Homicides committed by the young represented .05 percent of youth crimes. Still, the fifty-four homicides reached their highest peak since such data was first collected in 1961. The fifty-four killings involved seventy-two boys and twelve girls. Knives were used in 44 percent of the killings and firearms in 17 percent.

Appleby stated, "The Statscan report noted that in more than half of 2006's youth homicides, multiple perpetrators were involved. That compares with only 15 percent of the homicides in which adults were accused.... Peer pressure is a major factor in youth violence in the view of Constable Mills." (See the discussion on bullying in chapter 3.)

ANOTHER REPORT ON YOUTH VIOLENCE

The Statistics Canada data on youth violence cited above was gathered from police forces throughout Canada. It suggests a low level of violence by or against teens. However, another 2008 study, sponsored by Ontario Premier Dalton McGuinty, seemed to indicate otherwise.

Roy McMurtry and Alvin Curling headed the study. McMurty was the former Ontario attorney general and Curling was chief justice of Ontario, former speaker of the Ontario Legislative Assembly, and the first African-Canadian to hold a cabinet-level position.

The study was ordered in 2007 following the shooting death of a fifteen-year-old African-Canadian student in his Toronto school. Shortly after the killing, police arrested and charged two seventeen-year-olds with the murder. The killing apparently arose out of a fight. There did not appear to be any direct link to racism.

Still, the report stated, "We were taken aback by the extent to which racism is alive and well and wreaking its deeply harmful effects on Ontarians and on the very fabric of this Province."

Among the report's recommendations were: (1) that the province continue to press the federal government for a ban on handguns and (2) that community neighbourhood hubs be built for young people. This second approach envisions getting schools to assume a larger role in community youth development. The cost was estimated at $100 million (Alphonso 2008).

Help did come to the school where the teenager had been shot. Acting principal Jim Spyropoulos said, "The [school board] has been amazing.... We talk a lot about wraparound supports [for students]. You want to talk about wraparound? [The school] has got wraparound love — from facilities, from employee services."

The school was provided with two additional full-time hall monitors (for a total of four) and another vice-principal (for a total of three). Money came to beef up the library, and a new construction shop was approved. "We're fortunate that the people who are in the [new] roles have a really good grasp on the school and on the community," Spyropoulos said of the monitors and vice-principals (Rushowy 2007).

"PRESUMPTION" UNDER THE YCJA— BURDEN OF PROOF

Who has the burden of proving presumption under the YCJA? Under the YCJA, as a principle, young persons are presumed to have diminished moral responsibility (culpability). But, what does this presumption mean?

Another way of giving meaning to presumption is to state that the Crown continues to carry the burden of proof. Justice Abella wrote:

> Like all presumptions, it is rebuttable. Under the presumptive offences sentencing scheme, it is the young person himself or herself who is required to prove that the presumption should *not* be rebutted, rather than the Crown who is required to show why it should be. The constitutional implications

of this reversal of the onus create the legal knot we are asked to untie. To do so, we must first determine whether the principle of a presumption of diminished culpability is one of fundamental justice within the meaning of section7 of the Charter.

CHALLENGE QUESTION

A MATTER OF PRINCIPLE

Justice Abella reviewed the history of Canadian criminal law relating to young offenders. She noted that, on occasion, Parliament changed and made more restrictive both the liability and periods of custody imprisonment for young offenders. For example, she wrote of the then Young Offenders Act (YOA):

> Initially, section 16 of the YOA permitted the transfer to adult court of youths charged with the most serious offences. The Crown, in applying for such a transfer, bore the burden of demonstrating that it was appropriate. In *The Queen v. M. (S.H.)*, [1989] 2 *Supreme Court of Canada Reports* 446, this Court held that this was not a "heavy onus." Nor did the Crown have to demonstrate "exceptional" circumstances to make its case for transfer. Nonetheless, the Court noted "that is not to say that the transfer of a case from Youth Court to ordinary court is not a matter of the utmost seriousness."

The test for transfer was whether the judge was "of the opinion that, in the interest of society and having regard to the needs of the young person, the young person should be proceeded against in ordinary court." A number of factors were to be considered before transferring the young person, including the seriousness and circumstances of the offence, the young person's situation, and whether he or she already had a record.

In 1992, the federal government amended the YOA to lengthen the maximum sentence in youth court for murder from three years to five years less a day. It also amended the transfer provisions to stipulate that the "protection to the public" was the paramount consideration. The period of parole ineligibility was, however, reduced for young persons convicted of first and second-degree murder in adult court so that once incarcerated in adult facilities, they could be released sooner than their adult counterparts.

In 1995, the YOA was amended by the addition of section 16(1.01) to require explicitly that 16- or 17-year-olds charged with murder, attempted murder, manslaughter or aggravated sexual assault be tried as adults in ordinary court, unless the young person or the Crown applied to have the matter proceed in youth court.

The constitutionality of this provision was never tested in this Court.

Q: *If Parliament was able to change the law relating to penalties for young offenders, including violent young offenders, how can it be said that their diminished responsibility has some overriding legal principle that has held true over the years?*

The answer, in part, may come from the definition of *principle*, which includes the element of basic truth or assumption. In this regard, Justice Abella, before reciting the then new penalties, especially for violent youth crimes, noted the purpose of the YOA. She referred to section 3(1) of that act:

It is hereby recognized and declared that

(a) while young persons should not in all instances be held accountable in the same manner or suffer the same consequences for their behaviour as adults, young persons who commit offences should nonetheless bear responsibility for their contraventions [violations] ...

(c) young persons who commit offences require supervision, discipline and control, but, because of their state of dependency and level of development and maturity, they also have special needs and require guidance and assistance.

Justice Abella, again speaking for the majority of the Supreme Court of Canada, found in the current law, in section 3(1) of the YCJA, a carry-forward of that legislative purpose:

The following principles apply in this Act:

(b) the criminal justice system for young persons must be separate from that of adults and emphasize the following:

(i) rehabilitation and reintegration,

(ii) fair and proportionate accountability that is consistent with the greater dependency of young persons and their reduced level of maturity,

(iii) enhanced procedural protection to ensure that young persons are treated fairly and that their rights, including their right to privacy, are protected.

Justice Abella wrote that "section 3(2), moreover, states that the YCJA 'shall be liberally construed so as to ensure that young persons are dealt with in accordance with the principles set out in subsection (1).'" She added, "The preamble [of the YCJA] recognizes society's 'responsibility to address the developmental challenges and the needs of young persons and to guide them into adulthood;

encourages guidance and support; and seeks effective rehabilitation and reintegration.'"

In summary, the facts seem to be that Parliament, at one and the same time, chose to make the penalties, especially for violent serious crimes of young offenders, subject to greater penalties while also keeping as a central purpose of the law the principle of diminished culpability of young offenders.

POLICE PRESENCE IN HIGH SCHOOLS

In September 2008, a new program began in Toronto. A total of thirty police officers were assigned to thirty different high schools across the city (twenty-two in the Toronto District School Board and eight in the Toronto Catholic District School Board). Some critics predicted the worst. One public school trustee said, "To have them walking the halls and wearing guns in high schools, where guns are a problem, is mind-blowing to me."

But the critics, it seems, were wrong. At the high schools with a full-time police presence, attendance is up and suspensions and criminal charges are down.

Staff Sergeant Sharon Davis, who coordinates police officers in the School Resource Officer program, discussed the importance of the drop in criminal charges. She said, "Anybody who ends up needing to be arrested — that's a failure. Once young people enter the criminal justice system, all studies show that their chances of success in life — finishing school, having a good job — are diminished."

The success of the program has been in large part due to the good relationships that have been established between the police officers and the students. Officers have made an effort to get to know the students and become a part of the school communities.

The guiding principle has been that dealing with minor problems by means of warnings and no-nonsense advice can be more productive than dragging young people "into the jaws of the justice system."

Numerous other Canadian cities and jurisdictions have comparable programs (Appleby 2009a).

THE PUBLIC'S RESPONSE

When the police program in Toronto high schools was reported in the *Globe and Mail*, a number of people posted comments on the newspaper's website. Most expressed support for the program, but others expressed serious concerns. A sampling of opinions follows:

- "I am all for this. I am a high school teacher and the Calgary Board of Education had an officer in each of their high schools when I taught with them several years ago.... Students were often in the constable's office, chatting, getting advice, etc. I saw a marked change in how the students perceived the police and their role."
- "If I were a student going to one of these schools, I would be happy knowing that there was someone to help and possibly protect me."
- "What has happened to our society that we require police officers in school?"
- "Perhaps security guards at half the cost or more would make this a more effective program. Seemingly, it is primarily security that the police presence provides."
- "This program shows students that cops are just regular folks and can have a positive impact on lives.... No one is expecting that this program will suddenly make crime disappear from schools, but if it steers some folks away from bad choices and makes others

feel safer coming to school, which early results suggest are the outcomes, then it's an excellent program."

- "This should be seen as a temporary add-on but far more focus should be put into finding solutions to the cause of the issue of 'dangerous' schools. Hopefully these officers are first taking many courses prior to providing advice to kids. Placing individuals in positions of authority does not [guarantee] that they have all the answers for these kids (or correct ones)."

- "When I went to high school 10–15 years ago, we had many, many violent incidents occurring. We were on the news three times in my grade 9 year! The following year we had a new principal who came in, expelled all the troublemakers and brought in a police officer to walk the halls once or twice a week. Not to mention the other police who would occasionally drive through our parking lot talking to students.... Our school cleaned itself up within a year, essentially ridding itself of a gang problem. The fact that police were there when this occurred cannot be coincidence."

- "Hopefully by being proactive rather than reactive, the police presence may help some kids who would go bad from doing so and, in any case, provide a safer classroom."

- "This [program] makes a big difference to kids when the only time they usually see police is in squad cars or getting out to arrest someone."

- "If the Toronto school board were serious about reducing violence in schools, it would spend more money on special education, psychologists and social workers."

A police officer is a presence. How that person is viewed depends not only on how he or she sees their duty but also on how students, teachers, administrators, and parents view the police officer.

YOUTH OR ADULT SENTENCE FOR A YOUNG KILLER

On September 21, 2006, twenty-three-year-old Michael Oatway was sitting in the back of an Ottawa-Carleton bus, listening to music on his iPod. Suddenly, he was surrounded by S.M. and three friends. S.M. (not further identified because he was seventeen at the time) demanded, at knifepoint, that Oatway give him his iPod. Oatway refused, and was fatally stabbed.

S.M. was found guilty of first-degree murder on November 28, 2008, following a three-week trial. Following the verdict, prosecutors said they would be seeking an adult sentence for S.M.

Under the YCJA, if S.M. were sentenced as a youth, the maximum penalty for first-degree murder would carry a ten-year sentence, although an offender can only spend a maximum of six years in custody, with the remainder of the sentence to be served in open custody, meaning a halfway house or the offender's own home. If sentenced as an adult under the YCJA, S.M. would serve ten years in jail (minus the time spent in pre-trial custody).

There is a very important difference between the two sentences, however. If charged as a youth, S.M.'s name would never be made public, and five years after the end of his sentence, the conviction would disappear from his record. If sentenced as an adult, the conviction would stay with him forever. He would remain on parole for the rest of his life, and his name would probably be made public.

THE SENTENCING HEARING

S.M.'s sentencing hearing began on January 28, 2009. As a result of the Supreme Court's decision in *The Queen v. D.B.*, the burden of proving that he warranted an adult sentence rested with the prosecution.

The prosecutor called four of Oatway's relatives to deliver emotional victim impact statements. Then the parole officer discussed S.M.'s difficult childhood; his unsuccessful efforts to straighten out his life; and his manipulative, aggressive nature.

S.M.'S SENTENCE

On February 12, 2009, Justice Robert Maranger of Ontario Superior Court ruled that S.M. should be sentenced as an adult and that the seriousness of the crime warranted the lifting of the publication ban on his identity.

S.M., now identified as Shawn McKenzie, was sentenced to ten years in jail. He would be able to apply for parole in seven-and-a-half years, however, because of the two-and-a-half years spent in custody following his arrest. (With actual adult sentences, the minimum is twenty-five years behind bars before eligibility for parole.) He will remain on parole forever, and the conviction will remain on his record.

The judge took into account McKenzie's difficult childhood and positive attributes, but added:

> I can say that I found it troublesome that through-out the proceeding, he did not show any sign of remorse or regret for his actions. He did not even express remorse or regret when the victim impact statements were read in open court at the sentencing hearing.
>
> It could be simply false pride, as described by his counsel, or frankly, it could be the emotional detachment of a very cold-blooded individual.

What may have tipped the scales for Judge Maranger opting for an adult sentence was the testimony of probation officer Andre Sarazin, who told the court that as a professional and private citizen, he would be more comfortable if McKenzie were supervised for a longer period of time.

The judge concluded, "I am not reasonably assured that Shawn McKenzie can be rehabilitated and reintegrated safely into society through a youth court sentence."

SOLUTIONS TO YOUTH VIOLENCE

Some criminologists who study youth crime believe that: (1) the worst offenders often come from the poorest families in the worst neighbourhoods; (2) they often have neglectful or absent parenting; and (3) the solution, if there is one, must come early, in the form of prevention programs.

Elliott Leyton, an anthropologist who has studied youth crime, believes that the solution to youth crime "lies in the reduction of unemployment, the increase in social programs and the use of punishment rather than prison." He expresses concern, however, about "the generation of vipers ... already created, those juveniles and young adults, some on probation, who have little if any feeling for others and are perfectly willing to slaughter the innocent." And, he asks, "Why is the entire system focused so heavily on the needs and rights of violent men and women?"

Leyton sums up what a smart society and justice system would do: "Radically improve social conditions and economic opportunities. Ruthlessly repress violence" (Blatchford 2009a; 2009b; 2009e; Seymour 2008; "Teen Sentenced as Adult in Michael Oatway Murder" 2009).

AN ADULT SENTENCE FOR
A "PUPPET MASTER" KILLER

On New Year's Day, 2008, fourteen-year-old Stefanie Rengel opened the front door of her Toronto home and faced a killer. She was stabbed six times and bled to death shortly after in the arms of a stranger who saw her staggering along the sidewalk.

Within hours, police arrested a seventeen-year-old male (identified as D.B.) and a fifteen-year-old girl (identified as M.T.) and charged them with first-degree murder. (Their identities were protected under provisions of the YCJA.) D.B. was alleged to have been the person who attacked Rengel. M.T., though not alleged to have been at the scene of the crime, was alleged to have been the "mastermind" behind the killing.

At M.T.'s trial, the court heard that she was obsessively jealous of Rengel, whom she had never met but regarded as a rival. For over eight months, through conversations, text messages, Facebook ramblings, and Internet chats, she used sexual blackmail to pressure D.B. to kill Rengel.

The jury considered thousands of pages of text messages between M.T. and D.B., including conversations that apparently detailed their plans for the murder. M.T., in explicit terms, threatened to cut off sexual relations with D.B. unless he killed Rengel. She warned him that she would break off with him completely. In one message, she had told him: "I want her dead.... We've been through this." Later, she added: "If it takes more than a week, then we're jus gonna be friends."

THE JURY DECIDES

The jury watched two videotaped statements given by M.T. to police just hours after being arrested. In both, she seemed emotionless. She acknowledged that, though D.B. was more violent, she was the one more committed to Rengel's death. She was asked by police, "He wouldn't have thought of killing her had you not been so upset about what you perceived as her interference in your relationship, right?" She answered simply, "Yes."

Prosecutors relied on a well-established legal principle: Counselling others to kill makes a person guilty of murder. On March 20, 2009, the jury found M.T. guilty of first-degree murder. It was then up to the judge to determine whether M.T. would be sentenced as a youth or an adult.

THE MEDIA'S RESPONSE

Following the jury's decision, the *Globe and Mail* published the following editorial:

> Sentencing a 15-year-old girl to an adult penalty, even for first-degree murder, is a major step for Canadian justice. The adult penalty is a mandatory life term. But it is the right step in the case of the Toronto girl known as M.T., convicted last week and awaiting sentence for her role in the stabbing death of 14-year-old Stefanie Rengel.
>
> Canada's courts tend to look assiduously, as they should, for any hope of rehabilitation in the young. But the adult penalty for those 17 and under has a special parole clause. At age 15, M.T. would be eligible for parole after five to seven years, at the trial judge's discretion. This is a built-in form of leniency, a promise that those who deserve a chance at rehabilitation can get that chance while they are still young. It is not really an adult penalty, but a hybrid of the adult and youth penalties. And it fits these circumstances.
>
> The killing of Stefanie Rengel was not a crime of passion, a "mistake" in judgment which might be blamed on youthful immaturity. Its cold-bloodedness chills the spine. For months, over countless emails, text messages and cell-phone conversations, M.T. urged her 17-year-old boyfriend to kill Ms. Rengel, a girl she had never even met, on the apparent basis of a grudge she had developed against her. (The boyfriend is about to be tried for first-degree murder.) When he said he might be recognized, she told him to cut leotards and put them over his face. When the

boy missed an earlier deadline for the killing, she withdrew sexual favours. When it was done, she re-enacted the killing with the boyfriend. Later, she protested to police that she and the boyfriend had talked of mundane things, in addition to the killing, as if that made her less of a killer.

None of this takes the onus off the boy who allegedly stabbed Ms. Rengel six times on New Year's Day, 2008, leaving her to bleed to death in agony, with only a kind passerby to comfort her. But it does mean that M.T., who was nearly 16, is a serious threat to public safety.

Will that threat be diminished by the time six years is past, the maximum term in custody (followed by four years supervised in the community), if she is sentenced as a youth? Will she be safe to release? It's impossible to predict at this point. No presentencing hearing has been held, and so it is not publicly known what sort of home life she has had, and what mental difficulties she might have experienced. But it is hard to see how her personal background would help the court predict the danger she poses. In these circumstances, the community's protection should be paramount.

With a life penalty, M.T. would have to demonstrate to a parole board that she is an acceptable risk for release. Perhaps in five to seven years — let's hope it's at least six — she will not be ready. But perhaps in 10 or 12 she will be. Perhaps, too, she needs the threat of life behind bars to force her to deal with whatever made her wish to kill in cold blood. Who is helped by treating her as a youth? Not her. Not society.

A life penalty has three other benefits: She will have to report to parole authorities for life, rather than be unsupervised after 10 years; the crime will not be erased from her record (if she ever winds up in adult court again) if she is crime-free for five years after a youth sentence would end; and finally, the penalty will be commensurate with the terrible crime she committed. To steal a young teenage girl's life from her for no other reason than some twisted self-gratification is monstrous, and requires a strong response that demonstrates the value this society puts on life ("Cold Blood and Adult Penalties" 2009).

THE JUDGE'S DECISION

On July 28, 2009, after a three-week jury trial and a one-week sentencing hearing in which two psychiatrists testified about their examinations of her, M.T. was sentenced by Justice Ian Nordheimer as an adult for manipulating her boyfriend into killing Stefanie Rengel. She lost her anonymity and was identified as Melissa Tordorovic.

Psychiatrists indicated that Todorovic's personality would not be fully developed until she was in her mid-twenties. Until then, they were reluctant to make a diagnosis. And, absent a diagnosis, let alone treatment, her future dangerousness was unknowable and unpredictable. The judge said that the sum of psychiatric evidence was that there was "some risk of a repetition of this conduct. While the precise degree of risk is unknown, the nature and extent of Melissa's role in this incident is cause for concern."

Justice Nordheimer said that "the puppet master is more culpable than the puppet."

THE SENTENCING OF D.B.

On September 17, 2009, Stefanie Rengel's actual killer was sentenced. The youth had pleaded guilty to first-degree murder in April 2009.

D.B. was four days short of his eighteenth birthday when he stabbed Rengel on January 1, 2008. The timing was crucial. An adult committing the same crime would receive an automatic life sentence with no parole for twenty-five years. "He bought himself 15 years right off the top," noted crown attorney Robin Flumerfelt, who emphasized the planning that had gone into the murder. "This had been planned and deliberated for months," said Flumerfelt. "It was not an impulsive act. It was a calculated scheme."

Stefanie Rengel's thirteen-year-old brother, Ian, made a victim impact statement at the hearing. He said, "Being four days shy of eighteen shouldn't mean automatically knocking fifteen years off the sentence for first-degree murder. My sister Stefanie didn't even get to live fifteen years."

Judge Ian Nordheimer sentenced D.B. as an adult. He has now been identified as David Bagshaw, and his photograph has been released (Blatchford 2009c; 2009d; 2009f; "Cold Blood and Adult Penalties" 2009; "Evil Must Be Taken Into Account" 2009; Small 2009; "Teen Guilty of 1st-Degree Murder in Death of Stefanie Rengel, 14" 2009).

REFERENCES AND FURTHER READING
* Cited by the Supreme Court of Canada.

Alphonso, Caroline. 2008. "Youth Violence Tied to Racism, Report Says." *Globe and Mail*, November 14.

Anand, Sanjeev S. 1999. "Catalyst for Change: The History of Canadian Juvenile Justice Reform." 24 *Queen's Law Journal* 515.*

Appleby, Timothy. 2008a. "Youth Homicides Up 3 Per Cent in 2006." *Globe and Mail*, May 17.

_____. 2008b. "Report Seeks $100-million for Youth Programs." *Globe and Mail*, November 14.

_____. 2009a. "Police Presence in High Schools Makes the Grade." *Globe and Mail*, February 5.

_____. 2009b. "Sentenced to Life, Gunman in Creba Slaying Unmasked." *Globe and Mail*, April 25.

Bala, Nicholas. 1990. "Dealing with Violent Young Offenders: Transfer to Adult Court and Bill C-58." 9 *Canadian Journal of Family Law* 11.*

_____. 1994. "The 1995 *Young Offenders Act* Amendments: Compromise or Confusion?" 26 *Ottawa Law Review* 643.

_____. 1997. *Young Offenders Law*. Concord, ON: Irwin Law.*

_____. 2003. *Youth Criminal Justice Law*. Toronto: Irwin Law.*

Bala, Nicholas, and Mary-Anne Kirvan. 2000. "The Statute: Its Principles and Provisions and Their Interpretation by the Courts." In *Juvenile Crime and Delinquency: A Turn of the Century Reader*, edited by Ruth M. Mann, 45. Toronto: Canadian Scholars' Press.*

Blatchford, Christie. 2008. "Creba Jury Delivers Stunning Guilty Verdict." *Globe and Mail*, December 8.

_____. 2009a. "How to Sentence Evil: As a Youth, or an Adult?" *Globe and Mail*, January 29.

_____. 2009b. "iPod Killer Gets Adult Sentence for Murder on Ottawa City Bus." *Globe and Mail*, February 13.

_____. 2009c. "No Remorse, No Mercy for Teenage 'Puppet Master'." *Globe and Mail*, July 29.

_____. 2009d. "Rengel Killer Gets Life for 'Truly Evil' Crime." *Globe and Mail*, September 28.

_____. 2009e. "A System Focused Too Heavily on the Rights of the Violent." *Globe and Mail*, January 30.

_____. 2009f. "Yes, These are Teenagers, But Murder Isn't a Phase." *Globe and Mail*, July 27.

"Cold Blood and Adult Penalties." 2009. *Globe and Mail*, March 24.

"Crown Seeks Adult Penalty in Creba Case." 2008. *Globe and Mail*, December 11.

Department of Justice. A Strategy for the Renewal of Youth Justice. Ottawa, 1998.*

DiManno, Rosie. 2009. "Creba Killer Gets Life — and a Name." *Toronto Star*, April 25.

Doob, Anthony, and Carla Cesaroni. 2004. *Responding to Youth Crime in Canada*. Toronto: University of Toronto Press.*

Doob, Anthony N., and Michael Tonry. 2004. "Varieties of Youth Justice." In *Youth Crime and Youth Justice: Comparative and Cross-National Perspectives*. Chicago: University of Chicago Press.*

Doob, Anthony, Voula Marinos, and Kimberly N. Varma. 1995. *Youth Crime and the Youth Justice System in Canada: A Research Perspective*. Toronto: Centre of Criminology, University of Toronto.*

"Evil Must Be Taken Into Account." 2009. *Globe and Mail*, July 29.

"Man, 20, Guilty of 2nd-Degree Murder in Jane Creba Shooting." 2008. *CBC.ca*, December 8.

Manson, Allan. 2001. *The Law of Sentencing*. Toronto: Irwin Law.*

"Regina Teen Sentenced as Adult in Good Samaritan Killing." 2008. *Globe and Mail*, November 28.

Rushowy, Kristin. 2007. "Last Spring's Slaying of Jordan Manners, 15, Was Catalyst for Change at Troubled High School." *Toronto Star*, December 26.

Sachs, Susan. 2008. "Report on Young Offenders Spurs Controversy in France." *Globe and Mail*, December 15.

Seymour, Andrew. 2008. "Man Found Guilty of First-Degree Murder in Oatway Killing." *Ottawa Citizen*, November 28.

"Sleight-of-Hand at the Supreme Court." 2008. *Globe and Mail*, May 17.

Small, Peter. 2009. "'No Sex Until Deed Done,' Rengel Trial Told." *Toronto Star*, March 20.

Sprott, Jane B. 1996. "Understanding Public Views of Youth Crime and the Youth Justice System." 38 *Canadian Journal of Criminology* 271.*

_____. 1998. "Understanding Public Opposition to a Separate Youth Justice System." 44 *Crime and Delinquency* 399.*

"Steinke Found Guilty of First-Degree Murder." 2008. *Globe and Mail*, December 5.

"Teen Gets Maximum Sentence for Medicine Hat Killings." 2007. *CBC.ca*, November 8.

"Teen Guilty of 1st-Degree Murder in Death of Stefanie Rengel, 14." 2009. *CBC.ca*, March 20.

"Teen Sentenced as Adult in Michael Oatway Murder." 2009. *CTV.ca*, February 12.

3

CHAPTER 3

BULLYING:
DEGREES OF HARM

Bullying is unwanted, aggressive behaviour that involves an imbalance of power between the bully and victim. It is an attempt to inflict intentional harm on another and it may occur repeatedly. Often that attempt is carried out in a series of acts, such as harassment on the Internet (cyberbullying). Often, the acts of harassment are carried out by a group formed for that purpose. The end goal, as noted, is to inflict harm — to see the target hurt.

Bullying often takes place at school as a manifestation of problems germinating both outside and inside the school. A large number of youth are bullied: estimates indicate that one in five Canadian children are victims of bullying, and one in twelve students find themselves harassed on an ongoing basis. (*http://www. child-abuse-effects.com/child-abuse-statistics.html*)

Most young bullies are never brought before the criminal justice system. Some become known to parents and school authorities, who implement their own sense of what "justice" requires — such as an open assembly discussion or even school expulsion. Also, more family doctors (and pediatricians) are becoming involved in preventive bully action plans.

The school system itself has on occasion been implicated in bullying behaviour — such as at sporting events where some players see an open invitation to punish the opposition. The line between what society will permit and what the criminal law will condemn can be crossed. We will discuss one high school sporting event that resulted in the death of a player. The central question then became: What was the role of the criminal law where the act, resulting in death, took place on a playing field during a school event?

Other laws have been enacted that are designed to curb young offender behaviour, such as Ontario's Parental Responsibility Act. This act states that under certain circumstances, parents of young offenders who (often as part of a group) have damaged or destroyed property may be taken to small claims court and held accountable up to $6,000. We will set out similar laws in other jurisdictions and the measure of their effectiveness in combating youth crime.

Among the questions raised in this chapter are:

- Is there always a rational explanation for bullying?
- How do students respond to bullying among class-mates?
- What is the responsibility of parents for their children's delinquency?
- Should cyberbullying be a criminal offence?

THE MURDER OF REENA VIRK

On November 14, 1997, Reena Virk, age fourteen, was lured to a quiet park in Victoria, British Columbia, where she was swarmed, brutally beaten, and killed by a group of seven girls and one boy, aged between fourteen and sixteen. Her body was found a week later submerged in water under a bridge. The cause of death, according to the pathologist, was not drowning. Rather, it was the beating and the injuries she had sustained, which the pathologist testified, were similar to "those which would result from a car being driven over a body."

The autopsy was able to determine that Virk had been kicked in the head eighteen times and beaten about the body so severely that tissue was crushed between the abdomen and the backbone. The attack itself came in two stages. First was a severe beating from which Virk tried to flee. She was caught and dragged underneath a bridge. There, the second phase of the attack took place. Her forehead was burned with a cigarette. Attempts were made to cut her hair. Her head was held in the water, and there was evidence that one of the group delivered a karate chop to Virk's windpipe.

REASONS FOR THE ATTACK

It was clear that some of the attackers were angry with Virk. One teen claimed that Virk had spread rumours about her. Another said that Virk had sex with her boyfriend. But, for all the investigation and the trials that later occurred, there was no single reason for the swarming. It is questionable that Virk willingly would have gone to meet the other teens if she had reason to fear for her safety.

THE LEADERS OF THE ATTACK AND THEIR TRIALS

According to the evidence, fifteen-year-olds Kelly Ellard and Warren Glowatski led the attack. Both were bound over to adult court for trial. Neither had any long-term relationship with Virk; based on the evidence, their relationship with Virk could be called brief, at most. Glowatski was tried first, and he was found guilty of second-degree murder. He was given a life sentence with the possibility of parole no earlier than seven years thereafter.

Glowatski had been abandoned by his father, and his mother was an alcoholic. He lived with a friend and was described as "mean," especially when he was drunk. Glowatski described himself as a gang member. He was called upon to testify at Ellard's trial, but he refused to do so. His reason: His sentence was under appeal. And perhaps more to the point, he feared for his own life if he testified.

Ellard was seventeen at the time of her first trial, which concluded two years after the fatal attack on Virk, and was found guilty of second-degree murder. She was given a prison sentence in April 2000 that made her eligible for parole in five years. At the time of sentencing, the trial Justice Nancy Morrison said:

> Kelly, you are young and intelligent and you have a wonderful family…. They believe in you and I can only say that you should never let them down…. You owe it to Reena Virk to live a life that is exemplary and you owe it to yourself…. Kelly has an overwhelming love of animals. She is gentle and caring with them. She is a gentle and shy person. She has never been in trouble, before or since…. She may have a chance to become a worthwhile and productive citizen.

Ellard had no history of trouble with the police or the youth court. Yet the evidence of her role in the attack on Virk included this testimony: It was Ellard who crushed a lit cigarette into Virk's forehead and punched her head at least twenty-five times. Another witness said that Ellard pushed Virk's head into a tree and pulled her into the water and held her there (Simmons 2000).

The first trial was not the end for Ellard. Her conviction was appealed. Her defence counsel argued that the Crown's cross-examination had been unfair, and the British Columbia Court of Appeal agreed. A new trial was ordered and it was held in 2004. The jury was deadlocked. Media reports indicated that, but for a single juror, Ellard would have been found guilty. This resulted in a third trial. The jury deliberated for five days and brought back a decision that would have sentenced Ellard to life in prison with no chance of parole until she had served seven years.

There then came another appeal from Ellard's defence lawyers, who argued that the trial judge failed to instruct the jury properly, and that certain evidence was not given proper weight. By a 2-1 vote, the British Columbia Court of Appeal agreed, and a fourth trial was ordered. This time, however, the Crown appealed.

By an 8-1 vote, the Supreme Court of Canada restored Ellard's conviction. Speaking for the majority, Justice Rosalie Abella said that even if the trial judge was in error, there was no reasonable possibility that it would have affected the verdict of guilty (Makin 2009).

Ellard, initially housed in a youth detention facility, has been involved in inmate assaults while incarcerated, including a group attack on a vulnerable person. At no time has she expressed any regrets to the Virk family. Having already served seven years, and now in an adult prison, she soon will be eligible for parole. In this regard, the parole officials are not required to release her. They will review her prison record, among other matters. It will be possible for her to be held in prison for several more years.

Glowatski, in the meantime, served his seven years mandatory prison term. He apologized to the Virk family and, by 2009, was on parole working in the Vancouver area.

In 2009, the Virk family, who witnessed the Ellard trials, apparently were getting on with their lives. As a way of dealing with grief, Virk's father wrote a book about his daughter's early years (Virk 2008). He said he wanted to "set the record straight." Following the murder, the Virks often spoke in elementary and high schools sharing their daughter's story. Mrs. Virk said, "Our main message is: When someone is being bullied, or you're being bullied, speak out about it because if one person had made a phone call … things could have been very different. Kids learn from that story" (Armstrong and Makin 2009.)

The Virks' emphasis seemed to be on preventive action — what individuals could do to stop more serious harm from occurring.

It seemed that the judicial system was not central to the means for obtaining justice. Virk's father said, after a fourth trial was ordered of Kelly Ellard (and before the Supreme Court of Canada set aside that order and restored her conviction), "I think we want to wash our hands of this now and live our life.... No more do I want to place any trust in this system.... It has become like a sad joke" (Mickleburgh 2009).

OTHER TRIALS AND SENTENCES IN THE CASE

The remaining six teens were tried and either found or pleaded guilty in individual youth court trials where they were charged with assault causing bodily harm. Their identities were shielded under the then Young Offenders Act. But the sentences handed down by the youth court judge were: one year, nine months, six months, one year probation, and one stayed and one conditional sentence.

There was a history of violence among the six teens. Their identity is referred to by letters, since publication of their names was prohibited:

- A., age fifteen, pleaded guilty to a charge of assault causing bodily harm to another girl at the same time as sentencing in the Virk trial. At the time of the second assault, A. was taking a mandatory anger management course at her school. The reason: She had punched a fellow student. A. saw herself as a friend of Ellard and Glowatski. While Glowatski was in jail, A. accepted collect calls from him.
- B., age fifteen, saw herself as A.'s best friend. B. said she was drunk the night Virk was murdered. The trial judge gave B. a choice of house arrest — if she agreed to have no contact with A. The alternative was close custody, that is, institutionalization. B. chose close custody.

- C., age fifteen, thought Virk had spread rumours about her. C. lived in a group home. The trial judge said that C. had "all the elements, quite frankly, of sociopathic conduct." C. showed no remorse.
- D., age fifteen, lived in the same group home as C. She had a lengthy record of assaults, theft, and breaches of probation. She was angry at Virk for allegedly having sexual relations with her boyfriend.
- E., age fourteen, had tried to set Virk's hair on fire.
- F., age fifteen, knew Virk. Apparently, she attempted to have the beating stopped. F. did this at a point when she felt Virk had "had enough."

(Moore 2000a)

FIGHTING BACK: STUDENTS TO THE RESCUE

Ninth-graders from Ontario's Keswick High School were in a heated game of speed ball in the school gym when one of the players, angry and unprovoked, shouted at his opposite number, Jack Kang: "You fucking Chinese." He then punched him in the mouth. Jack, of Korean descent and holder of a black belt in tae kwon do, responded with a punch that broke his assailant's nose. (Jack's father was a master of tae kwon do, and Jack himself taught children at his father's studio.)

The assailant, bloodied, dropped to his knees. Jack tried to comfort him. Both boys apologized, but that was not the end of the matter. Police school resources officers laid an assault charge against Jack the morning after the fray. They did so without interviewing witnesses, though they were aware of the racial slur — a matter that they simply put aside.

Police visited the home of Jack's assailant. Both the boy and his father said they didn't want to press charges because they didn't want to "ruin anyone's life." (Both boys were honour students with 90 percent averages.) Still, charges were laid. Further, the school principal suspended Jack and, in a letter, stated that he would recommend his expulsion from all schools in the region.

A meeting was arranged. Jack and his classmate were present. Apologies again were made and they shook hands. The principal cancelled his suspension order and expunged the suspension notice from Jack's record. He also withdrew the recommendation that Jack be expelled from any regional high school, stating that the letter had been sent in error.

STUDENT RESPONSE

Students at Keswick High School were aware of the incident and the discipline meted out. They responded by staging a walkout — four hundred students marched from the school protesting the criminal charge against Jack.

The student response got the attention of the media and, through it, the chief of police, Armand La Barge. He ordered another investigation under the direction of a senior hate crimes police unit. Thirty-five witnesses were interviewed. At a large media gathering called by La Barge, he stated that the initial investigation was not "as detailed as it could have or should have been." He recommended to the Crown that the charge against Jack be dropped. It was an action that the police themselves, in law, could not take.

The Crown agreed with him, and in open court, the charge against Jack was dropped. At one point, Jack's father, uneasy about the incident, thought of leaving the community. After the response of the students, and the reaction of the police and school, he decided to stay. He accepted the good wishes of the mayor who personally welcomed Jack's family to the community.

Jack's immediate community, at least in terms of the incident, was his school. His classmates were aware of the incident. They assessed the facts and acted quickly, and their action brought a peaceful and effective resolution. Jack and his classmate cannot be said to be friends. But it can be said that they are able to get along with each other (Friesen 2009a, 2009b; Swainson 2009).

RUGBY: BULLYING AND MANSLAUGHTER

The rugby game on May 2007 between two Mississauga, Ontario, high schools was heated. Manny Castillo, age fifteen, was the captain of his team from Lorne Park Secondary School. There was real competition between Castillo and a player from the opposing school — a major junior hockey player with an Ontario Hockey League team who had ambitions for professional status. Words were exchanged.

At one point, Castillo's opponent picked him up, flipped him, and drove him head-first into the ground. A referee testified that the opponent boasted that he had pile-driven Castillo as hard as he could. Castillo lay motionless on the ground. He died in hospital a few days later from head and spinal injuries.

CHARGED AND TRIED

Castillo's opponent, whose identity could not be revealed under the Youth Criminal Justice Act, was charged and tried for manslaughter. Defence lawyers argued (1) self-defence, as Castillo had a chokehold that the accused simply tried to break, and (2) that Castillo assumed the risk of injury when he became part of the game.

Ontario Justice Bruce Duncan heard the evidence and rejected the defences. He found the accused guilty of manslaughter. Players, he said, must obey the law and the codes for the conduct of games, including such contact sports as rugby. The response of the accused was in retaliation for the briefly held head-lock. Reading from a twenty-eight-page decision, Justice Duncan stated:

The playing field is not a criminal law free-zone. The laws of the land apply in the same way as they do elsewhere.... There was no justification in self-defence. Accordingly, the defendant committed an assault, an unlawful act. That unlawful act caused death. The defendant is therefore guilty of manslaughter.

The force applied by the defendant was not within the rules of the game.... Dangerous play inside or outside the rules is not acceptable.... The defendant intentionally applied force that was outside the rules of the game or any standard by which the game is played. Manny did not explicitly consent to that force, and I am satisfied beyond any doubt that no such consent can be implied.

SENTENCED

The Crown sought a two- to three-year sentence, opting not to seek an adult sentence. The defence sought a one-year probation.

On July 6, 2009, the Mississauga youth was sentenced to one year's probation, anger management counselling, and one hundred hours of community service. Castillo's father did not comment on the sentence but handed out copies of the victim impact statement he had delivered that morning in the hope that its message about organized sports would be communicated to the public. In the statement, he said, "I hope that organized sports, especially organized sports in schools, puts a no tolerance policy in place for violence and aggression in sports" (Cheney 2009; Mitchell 2009; Peat 2009; "Teen Guilty of Manslaughter in Rugby Death" 2009).

CHALLENGE QUESTION

THE EFFECT OF A MANSLAUGHTER
CONVICTION ON A SCHOOL SPORT

Q: Does the manslaughter conviction influence how rugby is to be played at the school level?

The rugby case was one of the Crown against a single person charged with violating the Criminal Code. The accused was found guilty. That was the end of the matter so far as the Crown's case under the Criminal Code was concerned. But schools, players, and parents were left asking how the conviction would affect the sport at the school.

Kieran Crowley, Rugby Canada head coach, said he had never heard of a death in rugby play prior to the incident involving Manny Castillo. Indeed, Doug Crosse, spokesperson for Rugby Canada, added that the manslaughter conviction would "confirm a lot of incorrect suspicions about the game." (The suggestion seemed to be that rugby might be seen as a game without rules.)

On the other hand, the verdict was seen by some as a way of realigning what should be the mark of acceptable athletic behaviour. Clayton Ruby, a lawyer recognized as a civil rights expert, said of the manslaughter conviction, "Some athletes have a skewed perception of acceptable behaviour. They think violence is part of sports, and these guys get away with it on a regular basis. A case like this serves notice" (Cheney 2009).

NEW RULES AND THEIR ENFORCEMENT

Educational authorities who allow school athletic competitions and set the rules for play and their enforcement are apparently reviewing the conviction handed down by Justice Duncan. Al Wolch, a former coach and, at the time of his quoted comments, a superintendent with the Toronto District School Board, said the decision of Justice Duncan will result in "significant" policy review concerning school athletics:

> We see incidents and injuries all the time
> — undercuts in basketball, kids running
> others to the boards in hockey and other
> episodes in football.... We have to look at
> educating better, but we also have to understand the people coaching are volunteers.
> Both have to go hand in hand or we may be
> better off not having certain sports.... We're
> always reviewing regulations. As you look
> at danger, you need to make sure coaches,
> responsible for these students, are qualified
> in theory as well as the technical and practical side (Grossman 2009).

In fact, the coaches and referees are much like the "police" on the field. The coaches can influence how the game is played, and the referees can enforce rules to prevent certain kinds of violence.

THE DOCTOR AND UNASKED QUESTIONS

It was a routine physical for the fifth-grade boy. The doctor was one the boy had known, and trusted, for several years. Toward the end of the examination, the doctor casually asked the boy his favourite subject. The answer: science. His patient had even won a prize at a science fair and was to go on and compete in a multischool fair.

But the boy was unhappy. He was being teased, jostled, and even occasionally beaten up by other students because of his success at the science fair. This was not a one-time event, but an ongoing pattern that could only be called bullying. The boy's mother wondered whether life wouldn't be easier if her son "just let the science thing drop."

The doctor had a sense of personal outrage. After all, he was a person of science, and he had worked hard to practice as a medical doctor.

PRESCRIPTION

The doctor encouraged the boy's mother to call her son's teacher and complain. And, he encouraged the boy to continue his love of science.

On reflection, the doctor noted what he did not say to his patient or to the boy's mother:

> And here are three things I now know I should have done: I didn't tell the mother that bullying can be prevented and that it's up to the school. I didn't call the principal or suggest that the mother do so. And, I didn't give even a moment's thought to the bullies, and what their lifetime prognosis might be.... Research has described long-term risks — not just to victims, who

are more likely than their peers to experience depression and suicidal thoughts, but to the bullies themselves, who are less likely to finish school or hold down a job.

So what should I ask at a checkup? How's school, who are your friends, what do you usually do at recess? (Klass 2009)

What the doctor suggested, as a part of routine examination, was greater medical involvement — of talking not only with his young patient's parents, but also with their teachers and principal. In effect, the doctor becomes part of a program to change the culture of a school. The doctor attempts to put in motion the kind of ongoing inquiry to get the facts of bullying and then to address those facts not simply in terms of the victim, but also, and perhaps more importantly, *activating the bystanders who in the past simply watched the harassment and walked on* [emphasis added].

CHALLENGE QUESTION

A DOCTOR'S TIME

Q: In the average appointment time of fifteen minutes, how can a doctor examine a patient, ask the questions relevant to bullying, and follow up if a problem is spotted?

Pediatricians and family doctors — indeed most physicians — have busy practices. Most physicians make a living as a result of the number of patients they see. Their time is limited. As a practical matter, it is difficult for a doctor to give any one patient more than a fixed amount of time.

Many medical schools specifically train doctors to be attuned to their patient's health through observation — questions as well as tests. Indeed, one hurdle the medical student must jump in Toronto (as in other medical centres) is to diagnose a test patient within fifteen minutes. Many medical students fail the test. Others identify accurately the problem within five minutes.

Five minutes would hardly suffice if the doctors were in practice. There would be tasks of prescribing, perhaps seeking specialist help, and asking the patient to return to see how the treatment is progressing. Identifying a bullying problem is not the same as developing a specific response and then following up to see that the problem has been resolved.

In June 2009, the American Academy of Pediatrics updated and expanded its policy on bullying. It suggested doctor involvement with, among others, parents and schools. It also developed readable brochures addressing specific aspects of bullying that doctors could place in their waiting rooms.

The following, taken from an introductory brochure, is a warning and a challenge, especially to parents who come with their children for a pediatrician check-up:

> While bullying has received increased media attention, there are still many misperceptions of this problem and its solutions.
>
> • Bullying is different than fighting or teasing. It is repetitive, negative actions by one person or persons against chosen victims.

- There are three groups of children involved: bullies, victims, and bystanders.

Bullying prevention is a highly researched and well-proven area of violence prevention. The social dynamics of bullying are similar in most settings — bullies begin the school year by picking on a large number of children. Those children whose emotional responses gratify the bullies become the chosen victims for the year. Victims are smaller and weaker (boys) or more socially isolated (girls) than the bullies. Since harassment rarely occurs overtly in the classroom, teachers may be slow to recognize the dynamics of bullying or to prevent it. Thus, parents should be counseled to discuss bullying prevention with school guidance counselors or administrators. While victims may be more likely to seek medical attention, long-term studies demonstrate that the poorest outcomes are among bullies themselves. Children labeled by their peers as aggressors or bullies at age 8 are more likely to end up incarcerated and are less likely to be steadily employed and in stable long-term romantic relationships by the time they reach age 30. Consequently, bullying prevention programs have a long-term benefit for both bullies and victims.

HOW TO USE THIS TOOL

- Since parents and children are concerned about bullying, leave this brochure in the waiting room.
- Ask the parents: *'Is your child picked on in school?'* When you discover a child is being picked on, discuss the specific strategies with parents. Parents should be advised to discuss bullying with the school guidance counselor and/or principal.
- This brochure is particularly useful as a handout for school and community groups.
- When faced with a child who has an unusual new onset of school phobia or attention problems, gently probe about being picked on or teased before, during, or after school. This child may have difficulty focusing on class work, be reluctant to attend school, or have a variety of psychosomatic conditions.
- Victims often internalize the criticism of bullies and feel that they deserve the teasing and may be ashamed.
- When the school has alerted parents that their child is aggressive or

a bully, insist that the child receive counseling and that the parents take the issue seriously.

When giving this brochure to their parents, note that bullies, especially male bullies, are at a high risk for poor long-term outcomes unless the bullying is stopped at a young age.

The reason why certain students become victims is not always as clear as the Academy might suggest. Sometimes it is simply a matter of happenstance. Sometimes they are chosen simply because they are, for example, new to the school. But this much is certain: they are unable to defend themselves from the taunts of others.

A central questions remains: How can schools establish an anti-bullying environment? A roving school police officer, like a constable on patrol (cop), might lessen the urge for violent behaviour. But, as we shall see, it will do little to thwart such harassment as cyberbullying. In a major article in *Pediatrics*, the journal of the American Academy of Pediatrics, the authors spoke of the role of teachers as an anti-bullying force:

Teachers play a key role in preventing and intervening with bullying at school, yet they receive little if any help or training in how to effectively deal with such problems. They lack information, and they are reluctant to intervene when they witness bullying. Although teachers have the benefit of understanding the social context of bullying, they do not necessarily know how to best use this knowledge to intervene. In school settings, bullying and victimization are often considered as personal problems of individual youth rather than problems requiring a collective response. Therefore, it is essential: (1) to educate teachers about ways in which schools can alter social norms toward bullying; (2) to assist them to intervene effectively with incidents of bullying; and (3) to work together with clinicians to deal with the symptoms of bullying and victimization (Juvonen 2003).

CHALLENGE QUESTION

PARENTAL RESPONSIBILITY

Q: What responsibilities should the law impose on parents in guiding and supervising their children?

Recognizing that citizens can influence the kind of laws enacted, what should be the public policies made into law affecting parents in their child-raising responsibilities?

In 2000, a new Ontario law expanded parental responsibility for property damage done by their children (those under eighteen). Under the law, it is assumed that such property damage was intentional — unless the child's parents can prove otherwise. The parent must also show that he or she made "reasonable efforts to prevent or discourage the child from engaging in the kind of activity that resulted in the loss or damage." The victim's remedy is through an action in small claims court with an upper limit of recovery of $6,000. To initiate such a suit, court fees of between $50 to $100 must be paid.

Manitoba has a parental responsibility law, but it is not one that sets up a presumption that the damage done by the child was intentional. And it should be noted that Ontario has had a law that declares that in "damage to property or for personal injury or death caused by the fault or neglect of a child who is a minor ... the onus [burden] of establishing that the parent exercised reasonable supervision and control over the child *rests with the parent*" [emphasis added].

Of the law, the *Globe and Mail* concluded, editorially:

> The parent must show that he or she made reasonable efforts to prevent or discourage the child from engaging in the kind of activity that resulted in the loss or damage. And, what are reasonable efforts? The law offers hints: attending courses to prove parenting skills, and seeking professional assistance for the child designed to discourage activity of the kind that resulted in the loss or damage.... Does this mean the usual advice and remonstrations of parenthood will count for little if parents haven't been to courses or sought professional assistance? ...

The Ontario government clearly hopes to kill two birds with one stone: to make it easier and faster for victims of malicious damage to receive compensation, and to force willfully negligent parents of young terrors to more actively monitor and address their children's misbehaviour. But the wording of the new law appears to put a greater, vaguer and unfair onus on all parents of children who damage property, and to encourage judicial inconsistency as the already overburdened courts try to figure out where to draw the new dividing line of liability ("Who's a Bad Parent, Then?" 2000).

The reality of parental control was noted by Anthony Doob, Centre of Criminology, University of Toronto, and Jennifer Jenkins, Department of Human Development and Applied Psychology, University of Toronto:

Canadian survey evidence from a representative sample of 10-year-olds and 11-year-olds suggests that it is a minority of parents who know about the misbehaviour of their children. In one study, only 30 percent knew their children had been questioned by police. As for children who reported that they had skipped school, only 20 percent of the parents knew this. Adolescents work hard at keeping their parents ignorant of certain aspects of their lives (Doob and Jenkins 2000).

OTHER APPROACHES: THE UNITED STATES

TRUANCY CONTROL

Public school officials and prosecutors in a number of states are working together to fight truancy by holding parents criminally responsible through a fine and/or jail. The problem of truancy is often seen as acute. In 1998, for example, 63,000 of Detroit's 180,000 public school students missed more than a month of classes. Parents of sixty-seven of the worst offenders were called in by officials and warned that they could be jailed if they did not get their children to school. In February 1999, six mothers in Springfield, Illinois, were charged with a misdemeanour for improperly allowing their children to miss school. They were liable for $500 fines and thirty days in jail (Meredith 1999).

CRIMINAL RESPONSIBILITY

Oregon enacted a law in 1995 allowing parents to be held criminally liable for the delinquency of their children. This could mean fines, jail time, or mandatory parenting courses. The law resulted from experience with an ordinance of Silverton, Oregon, where a curfew for young people had been in effect. The Silverton police chief, Randy Lunsford, said of the ordinance, "I don't think we're telling people how to parent. We're just giving them a tool to become better parents, trying to get at some of the parental apathy and neglect" (Egan 1995).

CRIME DATA ON YOUNG OFFENDERS

The individual stories of violent youth crime can be alarming. The Reena Virk story was one that remained in the media for the better part of a decade. But, there are other stories that go beyond the young preying on each other.

Residents of a Montreal North community, long seen as safe, were jolted when a sixty-seven-year-old woman was assaulted at a bus shelter late on a May night in 2009. She was attacked by three boys aged fifteen to sixteen. They beat here savagely — all apparently only for the purpose of taking her purse. Two of the three assailants were later captured by police. They faced possible aggravated assault charges.

Many residents of the area were frightened. They questioned whether they should change their pattern of living — whether it was safe to go out at night (Marotte 2009).

Yet, youth crime is not on the rise — at least according to 2006 Statistics Canada data. The homicide rate for those twelve to seventeen was three per 100,000 in 2006. This broke down to eighty-four young people charged in fifty-four killings. Statistics Canada noted homicides were responsible for just .05 percent of overall youth crime and less than one percent of all violent crimes in which a weapon was present in 2006.

This is not to say that youth crime is at minimal levels. It is only to say that, relative to years past, youth crime has not shown any significant increase. Putting aside traffic offences, about 180,000 young people were involved in some Criminal Code violation in 2006. Youth violent crime increased 30 percent from 1991. About 80 percent of such crimes involved common assault, the least serious of that kind of offence.

Does the data warrant laws that toughen the criminal sentencing provisions for youth? Nicholas Bala, professor of Youth Justice Law at Queen's University, said youth crime must be taken seriously. He added, however, that there are other approaches that might be more effective, such as improving access to mental health programs and youth employment programs. Professor Bala said that, "these kinds of programs are actually changing the lives of young people" (Bala 2009).

The overall rate of youth crime was down 6 percent compared to a decade earlier and 25 percent since the peak year of 1991. The rate climbed 3 percent between 2005 and 2006 (Lawrence 2008).

YOU BE THE JUDGE

A MATTER OF SENTENCING: DETERRENCE?

THE FACTS

John, age sixteen, had been found guilty of aggravated assault. He had been tried before a judge alone. The facts seemed clear. John had been a gang member since he was twelve.

To be initiated as a gang member, John had to rough up two seniors. It didn't matter that they gave him whatever valuables they had without resistance; they had to be beaten up. No mercy was to be shown. That was the gang's mandate for membership.

John met the gang's requirements. In a period of three years, he had assaulted and seriously injured seven seniors. His net cash return was slightly more than $85, but from his point of view, the minimal return didn't matter. He had done what was expected of him. He rose in the ranks of the gang. He was held up as a "model" for incoming gang recruits.

Police eventually caught up with John. His seventh victim, a ninety-year-old retired teacher, was able to describe him as her assailant. At John's trial, a number of his fellow gang members turned out in support.

At the time of sentencing, the judge stated:

> I have a range of sentencing I can impose
> for your crimes…. But, I must centre the
> fact that you are a gang member and that
> your crimes were designed to further your
> gang's activities…. I think it necessary to

consider the need to impose a sentence that falls at the more severe end of the sentencing scale.... Your sentence hopefully will serve to deter others, including your gang, and yourself from ever committing such crimes in the future.

THE ISSUE

Can deterrence be a factor in sentencing?

POINTS TO CONSIDER

- John was deemed a youth within the meaning of the Youth Criminal Justice Act (YCJA).
- However, he was tried before a judge alone. He could have elected for trial by jury.
- Nothing in the YCJA refers to deterrence as a consideration in sentencing, though the provisions for sentencing are substantial.
- The Crown argued that (1) the judge had an inherent right to consider deterrence in sentencing and, (2) in any event, deterrence should be implied as a consideration in sentencing.
- Throughout his trial, and at sentencing, John did not indicate any remorse for the crimes he committed.

DISCUSSION

The youth court judge was wrong. In a unanimous decision, the Supreme Court of Canada ruled that deterrence cannot be considered as an element in sentencing under the Youth Criminal Justice Act (YCJA). The decision, written by Justice Louise Charron, was based exclusively on an interpretation of the YCJA.

That is, the Court attempted to determine the meaning of the YCJA as applied to the question of deterrence. The Court did not try to determine whether deterrence was a worthwhile goal in youth sentencing. It made this determination both in terms of general deterrence and specific (or individual) deterrence. It did not matter whether the youth court sought to use deterrence as applied to the community, or deterrence as it might relate to the accused — preventing him from committing crime again.

Justice Charron stated, in part, that:

> Deterrence, as a principle of sentencing, refers to the imposition of a sanction for the purpose of discouraging the offender and others from engaging in criminal conduct. When deterrence is aimed at the offender before the court, it is called "specific deterrence," when directed at others, "general deterrence." The focus of these appeals is on the latter.
>
> General deterrence is intended to work in this way: potential criminals will not engage in criminal activity because of the example provided by the punishment imposed on the offender. When general deterrence is factored in the determination of the sentence, the offender is punished more severely, not because he or she deserves

it, but because the court decides to send a message to others who may be inclined to engage in similar criminal activity.

While general deterrence as a goal of sentencing is generally well understood, there is much controversy on whether it works or not. Those who advocate its abolition as a sentencing principle, particularly in respect of youth, emphatically state that there is no evidence that it actually works in preventing crime. Those who advocate its retention are equally firm in their position and, in support, point to society's reliance on some form of general deterrence to guide young people in making responsible choices on various matters, for example, about smoking, using alcohol and drugs and driving a motor vehicle.

The question whether general deterrence works or not is not the issue before this Court. Whether the principles for youth sentencing should include deterrence was a matter of considerable debate in the passing of this new legislation. Ultimately, the repeal or retention of deterrence as a principle of sentencing for young persons is a policy choice for Parliament to make. This Court's role on these appeals is to interpret the relevant provisions of the YCJA so as to determine what choice Parliament in fact made.

The YCJA introduced a new sentencing regime. As I will explain, it sets out a detailed and complete code for sentencing young persons under which terms it is not open to the youth sentencing judge to impose a punishment for the purpose of warning, not the young person, but others against engaging in criminal conduct. Hence, general deterrence is not a principle of youth sentencing under the present regime.

SPECIFIC DETERRENCE

Justice Charron continued, addressing the matter of specific, or individual, deterrence:

The YCJA also does not speak of specific deterrence. Rather, Parliament has sought to promote the long-term protection of the public by addressing the circumstances underlying the offending behaviour, by rehabilitating and reintegrating young persons into society and by holding young persons accountable through the imposition of meaningful sanctions related to the harm done.

Undoubtedly, the sentence may have the effect of deterring the young person and others from committing crimes. But, by policy choice, I conclude that Parliament has not included deterrence as a basis for imposing a sanction under the YCJA.

Justice Charron seemed to draw a line between the YCJA goal of rehabilitation of the young offender and specific deterrence. It is rehabilitation that the YCJA is directed toward, not specific deterrence.

CYBERBULLYING: WOUNDING FROM AFAR

A high school sophomore had a crush on a boy who showed no interest in her. Angrily, she turned to the Internet and sent an email to her friend. It contained a racist comment about the boy. The friend forwarded the message to the boy, who forwarded it to his friends.

The sophomore felt she had done no more than confide in a friend. But her email was instantly conveyed to much of the student body, and its contents became a subject for talk, gossip, and ridicule. She and her parents felt they were under pressure, and she left the school.

A parent, who was also a lawyer, said, "If she had said those offensive things to her friend on the phone, I have a feeling the friend wouldn't have called [the boy] and repeated what she said, and even if she had, I doubt it would have had the same effect" (Harmon 2004).

SPEWING HATE

At an elite boys' private school, a grade 10 student set up a chat board, open only to his classmates and grade 10 students at two other private schools, one of them a girls' private school.

However, it was not long before the chat board was hijacked by other students who started their own cyber rooms on the site with names such as "The Reichstag" and "Gas Chamber." Photos were posted of Nazi rallies and of Nazis torturing Jews. The Holocaust was glorified. (Yet, it should be noted that the site sent other messages that had no hate content.)

A student from the girls' private school became aware of the website. She and three of her classmates looked at it and posted a note to the server asking that the hate-filled content be removed. The response: The girl who initiated the complaint was called a "hook-nosed parasite" who "should be thrown into an oven with the rest of them" (Teotonio, 2004).

Investigation suggested that students running the hate site were not actually animated by anti-Semitism. (Indeed, one of the hate site managers was Jewish.) Rather, it might have been, as another student suggested, that the hate dispensers thought it was "funny to outdo one another by making grossly politically incorrect statements" (Alphonso and Friesen, 2005).

BULLYING OUTSIDE SCHOOL: ACTION AND REACTION

The messages described were not sent from school computers. The boys were students, but the questioned computer activity was done at home. Still, the schools, their student bodies, and the faculties got involved. (Indeed, the popular media reported the story.) The boys' school principal said, "I think in this particular case, given the severity of what we were dealing with, rather than hide behind the attitude of 'well, we're going to leave this to parents and it's their issue' … we just felt that there was a moral and an ethical reason to get involved in this."

The female students went to their parents, and to their principal who praised them — and did so in front of an assembly of students. (They also went to the computer server, reported the incident, and asked that the site be closed. Within hours the site was closed.) The girls' school principal said to her students in one of several assemblies,

> We want girls to have a voice…. We encourage
> you to take a stand and not be afraid to make
> a difference…. Four girls at [this school] also
> decided that they would not be bystanders last
> week, and we are proud of their courage in com-
> ing forward to do something about unacceptable
> material on a student-created website….
>
> When you hear of a fellow student being
> deliberately excluded, ridiculed or called
> names, or when you hear unkind rumours
> about someone, it is not a joke…. Each of you
> can play your part to make sure that, as a com-
> munity, we do not tolerate bullying of any kind
> (Black, 2005).

The boys' school principal also acted quickly. He expelled three boys for either posting offensive photos or for the hate reply sent to the girls. He suspended four other students for not stopping what they saw happening. The suspensions were from two to four days. The expulsions were for the remainder of the school year. Any attempt on the part of those expelled to return, the principal said, would be subject to school review.

The *Toronto Star* wrote that the incident had a broader lesson in terms of prejudice and tolerance. Editorially, it stated:

> Of course, some might argue, kids will be kids.
> That sometimes means acting impulsively and
> foolishly. But that does not mean that students
> who posted the images and messages should be
> let off lightly for their abhorrent expressions of
> hate. While the students, one of whom is Jewish,
> apparently did not commit the odious acts on
> school property, the schools have dealt with the
> incident swiftly and appropriately.

[The boys' school] has expelled the boy who posted the photos and the two boys who responded to [the girls'] complaints. Both schools have also held assemblies to educate students about anti-Semitism. That sends a message to all students at these schools that anti-Semitism will not be tolerated. It is the right message.

The incident also reminds us that Canadians must remain vigilant against expressions of hate.... Tolerance must be nurtured both at home and at school. Children must learn the troubling histories of the Holocaust, the slave trade, the internment of Japanese Canadians during World War II and other human-rights atrocities. More important, we all must be ready to stand up to bigotry and racism, wherever it confronts us ("Standing Up to Hatred," 2005).

THE CRIMINAL LAW AND CYBERBULLYING

Cyberbullying has not been made a criminal offence. Current laws do not provide police with all the tools needed to investigate online harassment. Such was the position taken in 2008 by the Canadian Teachers Federation (CTF). Emily Noble, CTF president, stated:

We feel there's not enough teeth in the Criminal Code right now for cyberbullying.... A lot of people get on the electronic medium and think they can send whatever emails they want and they're anonymous. The reality is we need to take responsibility and care for each other. We all have to treat each other with respect.

The internet is the new playground. So let's get some ground rules in terms of how we treat each other. Teachers would like to know they've got some backup, and they've got some support from parents, the community and decision-makers (Mahoney, 2008).

Applying the criminal law to web harassment, however, has some difficulties, especially as it relates to those under the age of eighteen. Contrary to what cyberbullies may believe, tracing their identities is possible. The difficulty comes from their youthful status under the criminal law. The Youth Criminal Justice Act might treat the intimidation or threatening of another as an offence. But the young offender's identity, for the most part, would be protected.

A Media Awareness Network Survey in 2005 found that 34 percent of Canadian students had been bullied, and 27 percent of those bullied were threatened over the Internet:

The anonymity of online communications means kids feel freer to do things online they would never do in the real world. Awareness Network research from 2005 shows that 60 percent of students pretend to be someone else when they are online. Of those, 17 percent do so because they want to "act mean to people and get away with it." Even if they can be identified online, young people can accuse someone else of using their screen name. They don't have to own their actions, and if a person can't be identified with an action, fear of punishment is diminished ("Challenging Cyber Bullying." *www. bewebaware.ca/english/cyberbullying.html*).

The problem may not be the need for new laws so much better police training to enforce existing laws. Such seems to be the message of Prime Minister Stephen Harper who said: "I think we've got to stop using the term bullying to describe some of these things. Bullying to me has a kind of connotation of kids misbehaving. What we are dealing with in some of these circumstances is simply criminal activity. It is youth criminal activity. It is sexual criminal activity. And it is often internet criminal activity" (Taber and Walton, 2013).

The reach of the law over cyberbullying could include existing offences such as sexual assault, child pornography (even when produced and shared by other minors), the sexual exploitation of children, criminal harassment (no matter what the medium), uttering threats, and intimidation.

Nick Bala, a Queen's University law professor and expert on youth crime, says that "investigations often founder for lack of computer acumen. Police need the expertise not only to identify the individual who posted a message or photo, but those who reposted and distributed it (Makin and White, 2013)."

"KICK A GINGER DAY": JUST A JOKE?

In November 2008, some Facebook groups picked up the idea of "Kick a Ginger Day" to target red-haired children. Lacking any objective cause, the reason seemed to be for fun. (It may be that the "idea," if such it may be called, came from an episode of *South Park*, a popular animated television show in which a character speaks to his classmates about the evils of "ginger kids." They are called "nasty" and "born with a disease.")

But, Kick a Ginger Day was not so much fun for the recipients. The activity spread throughout North America. In Prince George, British Columbia, a red-head was kicked eighteen times before being allowed to go on his way. In Flin Flon, Manitoba, an elementary school principal met with a worried mother concerned about the safety of her red-headed son. In Ottawa, a mother let her thirteen-year-old red-headed son stay home because he was afraid of what a day in school might bring from his class mates (Windgrove 2008).

NEO-NAZI ATTACKS: A GERMAN PENALTY

Germany has experienced a number of violent attacks — including murders — against foreigners, many from Africa. The attacks seemed to have dated from November 25, 1990, when rightists killed an Angolan. On August 30, 2000, Judge Albrecht Hennig was responsible for sentencing three young neo-Nazis who had beaten to death Alberto Adriano, age thirty-nine, a meat packer from Mozambique. They did this because of the colour of the victim's skin.

One of the three was an adult, the other two, sixteen years old, were sentenced as juveniles. The adult was given a life term, the most severe penalty under German law. The youths were given detention terms of nine years each, one year less than the maximum allowed under German law.

Judge Hennig stated, "[The attack] was the latest in a long series of attacks to which we must put an end.... We need the engagement of civil society.... We need a repeat of what the people in the east of our country did in the peaceful revolution of ten years ago, an involvement in the fight for what is right" (Cohen 2000a; 2000b).

REFERENCES AND FURTHER READING
* Cited by the Supreme Court of Canada.

Alphonso, Caroline, and Joe Friesen. 2005. "Jewish Pupil among Three Expelled." *Globe and Mail*, May 3.

American Academy of Pediatrics. "Bullying: It's Not OK." *http:// www.aap.org/connectedkids/samples/bullying.htm*

Appleby, Timothy. 2000. "Making Sure Myles Didn't Die in Vain." *Globe and Mail*, September 2.

Armstrong, Jane, and Kirk Makin. 2009. "The Reena Virk Murder." *Globe and Mail*, June 13.

Bala, Nicholas. 2003. "Understanding Sentencing Under the Youth Criminal Justice Act." 41 *Alberta Law Review* 395.

Barriere, Darlene. "Bullying." Child Abuse Effects. *http://www. child-abuse-effects.com/bullying.html.*

Beaulieu, Lucien.1988. "From 'Challenges and Choices' to 'A Climate for Change.'" In *Y.O.A. Dispositions: Challenges and Choices, a Report of the Conference on the Young Offenders Act* in Ontario. Presented by the Ontario Social Development Council. Toronto: Ontario Social Development Council.*

Black, Debra. 2005. "Racist Incident Offers Lessons." *Toronto Star*, May 3.

Brown, Dana. 2009. "School Suspensions Over 'Kick a Ginger' Anger Parents." *Toronto Star*, November 24.

Canadian Department of Justice. *YCJA Explained. http://www. justice.gc.ca.*

_____. 1999. *Youth Criminal Justice Act: A New Law —A New Approach*. Canadian Department of Justice: Ottawa.

"Canada Tougher on Crime than U.S." 2000. *National Post*, May 8.

Cheney, Peter. 2009. "Family, Friends Weep as Athlete Found Guilty of Manslaughter." *Globe and Mail*, May 29.

"Clark Unveils Tories' Tough Stand on Crime." 2000. *Globe and Mail*, September 1.

Cohen, Roger. 2000a. "Neo-Nazis Show No Remorse at Trial, and a German Widow Is Overcome." *New York Times*, August 23.

_____. 2000b. "3 Neo-Nazis Guilty of Immigrant's Murder." *New York Times*, August 31.

Cusson, Maurice. 1983. *Why Delinquency?* Translated by Dorothy R. Crelinsten. Toronto: University of Toronto Press.*

"Cyberbullying Should Be a Criminal Offence: Teachers." 2008. *CBC.ca*, July 12.

Doob, Anthony, and Jennifer Jenkins. 2000. "Loaded Dice in the Parenting Game." *Globe and Mail*, August 16.

Egan, Timothy. 1995. "If Juveniles Break Law, Town Is Charging the Parents, Too." *New York Times*, May 31.

Friesen, Joe. 2009a. "As Assault Charge Dropped, Jack Was Facing Another Test." *Globe and Mail*, May 14.

_____. 2009b. "Chief Urges No Charge in Schoolyard Punch-up." *Globe and Mail*, May 7.

Gadd, Jane. 2000. "Making Parents Pay Won't Work, Critics Say." *Globe and Mail*, August 16.

"Getting Out of Prison." 2008. *CBC.ca*, March.

Gray, Jeff. 2005. "School Probes Student Involvement in Anti-Semitic Internet Chat Room." *Globe and Mail*, May 2.

Grossman, David. 2009. "Rugby Case Stirs Debate for Schools." *Toronto Star*, May 29.

Harmon, Amy. 2004. "Internet Gives Teenage Bullies Weapons to Wound from Afar." *New York Times*, August 26.

Juvonen, Jaana, Sandra Graham, and Mark A. Schuster. 2003. "Bullying Among Young Adolescents: The Strong, the Weak, and the Troubled." *Pediatrics* 112 (December): 1231–37.

Klass, Perri. 2009. "At Last, Facing Down Bullies (and Their Enablers)." *New York Times*, June 6.

Lawrence, Daina. 2008. "StatsCan Reports Rise in Violent Youth Crime." *Toronto Star*, May 16.

Mahoney, Jill. 2008. "Criminalize Cyberbullying, Teachers' Proposal Urges." *Globe and Mail*, July 12.

Makin, Kirk. 2009. "Supreme Court Restores Ellard Conviction in Virk Case." *Globe and Mail*, June 12.

Makin, Kirk and Patrick White. 2013. "Parsons Case Provokes Larger Debate About the Law and Policing of Cyberbullying." *Globe and Mail*, April 13.

Marotte, Bernard. 2009. "Teens Held in Savage Beating of Woman, 67." *Globe and Mail*, May 19.

Martin, Sandra. "Murder in Victoria: Why Did Reena Virk Die?" *Chatelaine*, May 1998.

Meredith, Robyn. 1999. "Truants' Parents Face Crackdown Across the U.S." *New York Times*, December 6.

Mickleburgh, Rod. 2009. "Reena Virk's Family Stunned as 4th Trial Ordered for Ellard." *Globe and Mail*, September 6.

Mitchell, Bob. 2009. "Teen Guilty in Rugby Death." *Toronto Star*, May 28.

Moore, Dene. 2000a. "Girls Who Beat Virk Had Long Histories of Violence." Canadian Press, April 1.

_____. 2000b. "Testimony Virk Jury Didn't Hear." Canadian Press, March 29.

Peat, Don. 2009. "Probation in Rugby Death." *Toronto Sun*, July 6.

Roberts, Julian V., and Nicholas Bala. 2003. "Understanding Sentencing Under the *Youth Criminal Justice Act*." *Alberta Law Review* 41: 395–423.*

Simmons, Steve. 2000. "Teen Sentencing a Judicial Disgrace." *Toronto Sun*, April 24.

"Standing Up to Hatred." 2005. *Toronto Star*, May 4.

Swainson, Gail. 2009. "Charges Dropped in Racial Slur School Fight." *Toronto Star*, May 13.

Taber, Jane and Dawn Walton. 2013. "Bullying Can Be a Crime, PM Says as Halifax Vigil Honours Rehtaeh Parsons." *Globe and Mail*, April 11.

"Teen Guilty of Manslaughter in Rugby Death." 2009. *Globe and Mail*, May 28.

Teotonio, Isabel. 2005. "Anti-Semitism on Website Has Elite Schools in Uproar." *Toronto Star*, May 2.

Virk, Manjit. 2008. *Reena: A Father's Story*. Vancouver: Heritage House.

"Who's a Bad Parent, Then?" 2000. *Globe and Mail*, August 17.

Windgrove, Josh. 2008. "Kick a Ginger Prank Gets Police Seeing Red." *Globe and Mail*, November 21.

Wingert, Pat, and John Lauerman. 2000. "Parents Behaving Badly." *Newsweek*, July 24.

Zimring, Franklin E. 1981. "Kids, Groups and Crime: Some Implications of a Well-known Secret." 72 *Journal of Criminal Law and Criminology* 72, no. 3: 867–85.*

CHAPTER 4

POLICE SNIFFER DOGS:
SCHOOLS AND PUBLIC PLACES

A locker search might be carried out on a tip from another student; a random baggage search might be based on police-generated profiles. These searches can be aided by electronic devices or trained sniffer dogs. If, for example, illegal drugs are found, they no doubt will be seized, and there is the strong possibility that charges will be laid. If the illicit substance is found in a school, there is the added possibility of discipline, including suspension or expulsion.

Searches, however, whether of the person or the person's belongings, whether youth or adult, are an invasion of that person's constitutional rights. This invasion can be justified under the law, but there are conditions that must be met for such an invasion to be accepted and for the illegal item (drugs or weapons) to be used in support of any charge or penalty.

Among the questions raised in this chapter are:

- Is the police use of sniffer dogs to find illegal drugs a "search"?
- What is the importance of where the dogs are used?
- If the police dog signals illegal drugs, may police conduct a search?

- Does the Charter of Rights and Freedoms set standards for the use of police sniffer dogs?

Police have long used dogs as investigating "tools." Their noses have a sense of smell far more sensitive than those of humans. They have been used to find suspects where the only identification is a piece of clothing believed to have been worn by that person. They have also been trained to locate illegal drugs that, in turn, provide police with leads both to ferret out illegal drugs and arrest those engaged in trafficking.

This chapter focuses on two cases decided by the Supreme Court of Canada on the same day: April 25, 2008. In both cases, a Court majority (six of nine Justices) agreed that the evidence of illegal drugs found by police as a result of dog sniffing could not be used at trial.

The cases are *The Queen v. A.M.* and *The Queen v. Kang-Brown*. In both cases, the Attorneys General of Ontario, Quebec, and British Columbia were granted the right to intervene and argue before the Court. Others permitted to intervene in *The Queen v. A.M.* were the Canadian Foundation for Children, Youth and the Law, and the St. Clair Catholic School Board (where the police use of sniffer dogs took place at the invitation of one of its high school principals).

The cases present real difficulties as to the legal lessons we are to take away from the decisions. Bear in mind that the rulings of the Supreme Court of Canada are the law of the land. But when we say "rulings," we mean the reasoning that led the Court to its decision. It is the reasoning in support of a decision that makes a Supreme Court of Canada decision a precedent — that is, binding on the Court and lower courts.

In each of the two cases discussed in this chapter, there was a total of four decisions. The Court was polarized. Still, on some of the key issues, a majority of the justices did agree. To that extent, their reasoning and decision can be taken as precedent. However, we will also discuss the limitations that the justices imposed on themselves as to the scope of the conclusions reached.

All the justices seemed to agree that the issues were to be resolved not by any statute — for Parliament had not enacted any law to deal with the issues in dispute. Rather, the issues were to be resolved by "judge-made law," as it had been developed and applied by the Court itself. This, in turn, meant that the facts in any case were important. Any significant variation in facts could change the reasoning from one case to another. This had special meaning for the subject of searches.

The investigatory techniques might be the same as applied to adults and young persons. But, should the rules relating to the use of those techniques, as applied for example to sniffer dogs, be different for luggage searches at a bus station as contrasted to bag searches at a high school?

What we will do is describe the issues raised by the justices and how they dealt with them. Then, we will more clearly see where Court majorities exist and thus precedent has been set, and where there remain issues to be decided in future cases.

Here are the central issues raised and discussed in the two Supreme Court of Canada decisions:

- Against what standard are searches to be measured to determine their lawfulness?
- When can it be said that a search has taken place?
- Under what circumstances will a search be ruled "unreasonable"?
- Even if a search is unreasonable, is it possible to use the resulting evidence in a criminal trial?

The Queen v. A.M. will frame our discussion in this chapter. That case, along with *The Queen v. Kang-Brown,* will be discussed under the Charter of Rights and Freedoms, part of the Constitution of Canada. We will begin our discussion with the relevant Charter provisions and with the issues raised under them. This will be followed by a summary of the facts, the first part of which will deal with the nature of sniffer dogs. *The Queen v. Kang-Brown* will be developed in "You Be the Judge," challenge questions, and queries.

A STANDARD:
THE CHARTER OF RIGHTS AND FREEDOMS

SECTION 8 OF THE CHARTER

Under the Charter of Rights and Freedoms, the primary provision relating to search or seizure is section 8. It consists of a few words that, on their face, seem quite simple: "Everyone has the right to be secure against unreasonable search or seizure."

The meaning of those words, however, has caused much conflict. The courts have been called upon to define what is an unreasonable search or seizure. In the cases discussed in this chapter, for example, have dogs conducted a search by sniffing the air and reacting, having been trained to detect unlawful drugs? If the answer is yes, then the first step has been taken in requiring the police to obtain judicial permission for a search.

The words of section 8 of the Charter do not answer these questions. Up to this point, the courts have given meaning to the words of the Charter section. This task of interpretation derives from the courts' historic functions. It is the common law. The courts — and finally, and most importantly, the Supreme Court of Canada — look to past decisions and, generally slowly, case by case, graft meaning onto the words. Seldom is this done with any one sweep of a generalized decision.

And, certainly this is true of *The Queen v. A.M.* and *The Queen v. Kang-Brown*. One case involved a sniffing police dog that was walked round a school gym where students had placed their backpacks. The other related to police stopping a bus passenger and using a sniffer dog to walk alongside his luggage.

If there were any common approach to decisions involving search or seizure, it would be in factual detail insisted on by the courts in applying the language of section 8. Put differently, out of the facts the courts derive the meaning of the law.

SECTION 9 OF THE CHARTER

Section 9 of the Charter states, "Everyone has the right not to be arbitrarily detained or imprisoned."

Often when we think of searches or seizures, there is the image of police forcibly detaining an individual, while searching the person or that individual's property. In *The Queen v. A.M.*, police did not use such force. Students had piled their backpacks in the gym. Police, at the invitation of the school principal, walked a sniffer dog around the backpacks. It was in that setting that police found drugs.

In *The Queen v. Kang-Brown*, police spotted the profile of a suspicious person, one who might be a drug carrier. They walked a sniffer dog around his luggage where they later discovered a stash of unlawful drugs. Section 9 provides the standard to determine whether the use of trained police dogs in such a context amounts to a "seizure of personal property." At best, it is a generalized standard.

SECTION 24 OF THE CHARTER

Section 24 of the Charter states:

> 24(1) Anyone whose rights or freedoms, as guaranteed by this Charter, have been infringed or denied may apply to a court of competent jurisdiction to obtain such remedy as the court considers appropriate and just in the circumstances.

24(2) Where in proceedings under subsection (1),
a court concludes that evidence was obtained in
a manner that infringed or denied any rights or
freedoms guaranteed by this Charter, the evidence
shall be excluded if it is established that, having
regard to all the circumstances, the admission of it
in the proceedings would bring the administration
of justice into disrepute.

Assume that there has been an unlawful search or seizure.
What is the result? Bear in mind that the question is raised in the
context of a criminal proceeding. Often, the question is raised
when the Crown seeks to introduce evidence coming from the
search and seizure. In the cases examined in this chapter, the evidence is the illegal drugs that police found in the student backpack
or the luggage of the accused.

If the judge excluded the evidence because police obtained
it in violation of the Charter, then frequently the Crown's case
against the accused collapses.

Section 24 of the Charter specifically deals with evidence that
police obtain in violation of the Charter. That provision does not
deny the Crown the right to introduce the evidence and have a
judge and/or jury consider it in reaching a verdict. Rather, the
unlawfully obtained evidence cannot be used when "the admission
of it in the [court] proceedings would bring the administration of
justice into disrepute."

Again, the words of the section are general. They don't guide the
court as to when the administration of justice would be brought into
disrepute. Is the answer to be found in the seriousness of the police
violation, or is it to be discovered in the real danger of the crime that
has been prevented?

The courts must give meaning to the language of the Charter
provision. The scope of the Court's decision — how broadly it will
cast its reasoning — is, however, another matter. In *The Queen v.*

A.M., Justice LeBel, speaking for himself and two other justices, wrote, "Courts make and change the law.... Much of what is recognized as 'law' is actually, in one form or another, judge-made law.... The question is not whether this lawmaking power exists, but how and when it is appropriate to exercise the power."

CHALLENGE QUESTION

A ROLE FOR PARLIAMENT

Q: *Is the Supreme Court better able than Parliament to define when and how police are to use sniffer dogs?*

The Supreme Court can have a shared role with Parliament in defining when and how sniffer dogs are to be used by police. Justice Deschamps spoke of this, and her comments were not challenged by other members of the Court in either *The Queen v. Kang-Brown* or *The Queen v. A.M.* She said,

> Many decisions must be made about when and how dogs ought to be used in law enforcement, and both the public and the police are entitled to know how these animals can and will be used in Canada.
>
> This direction is best provided by Parliament, which is able to create a wholistic and harmonious scheme for the use of sniffer dogs in this country. Courts, on the other hand, are ill equipped to deal with the multitude of issues arising from the use of sniffer dogs.

Not only are judges restricted to considering the issues and factual scenarios placed directly before them by specific parties (and therefore unable to create a wholistic scheme regulating the use of dogs generally). They also do not have access to the expertise necessary to determine what type of training sniffer dogs should receive or what degree of accuracy they should have in order to be deemed "reliable."

Courts are also poorly positioned to determine when dogs should be used on bags as opposed to persons, when a warrant ought to be obtained prior to use of the dogs, and what form notice must take when sniffer dogs are used in a generalized way.

All of these important decisions are best left to Parliament, which can study the various aspects of sniffer dog use and craft policies suited for the Canadian context, in which Charter rights must be carefully balanced against the need for effective law enforcement.

Unfortunately, Parliament has remained silent on the use of sniffer dogs, and the courts must therefore evaluate police use of this tool, absent any statutory direction from this country's policy makers.

Parliament remains free to enact legislation even after the Court has stated its view. The Court's decision (or holding) relates to its reasoning and the principles embodied in that reasoning. This leaves it to the legislature to set out the details that would implement the standards. For example, the legislature could set criteria necessary for the qualification of a police dog as a sniffer. And, the legislature could say that the failure to use a properly qualified police sniffer dog would result in the evidence uncovered by the dog being treated as inadmissible.

THE COMPARATIVE SKILLS OF SNIFFER DOGS

Not all sniffer dogs are equally skilled at detecting illegal drugs. Justice Deschamps, in a concurring opinion joined by Chief Justice McLachlin, gave the Court a majority in ruling the search unlawful in *The Queen v. A.M.* She emphasized the differences between sniffer dogs and the need for police to demonstrate the sniffing skill of any particular dog whose alert is used as a basis for a search. Justice Deschamps stated:

> The evidence in this case is that the sniffer dog Chief has an enviable record of accuracy. Of course dogs, being living creatures, exhibit individual capacities that vary from animal to animal. While a false positive may be rare for Chief, it is not thus with all dogs. The importance of proper tests and records of particular dogs will be an important element in establishing the reasonableness of a particular sniffer-dog search.
>
> The Crown attaches considerable importance to what it says are statistics relevant to the

detection rate, that is to say the successful location of drugs in a search conducted pursuant to a dog sniff (true positives), but an important concern for the Court is the number of *false positives. From the police perspective, a dog that fails to detect half of the narcotics present is still better than no detection at all. From the perspective of the general population, a dog that falsely alerts half of the time raises serious concerns about the invasion of the privacy of innocent people* [emphasis added].

She went on to quote from a dissent of U.S. Supreme Court Justice Souter, who questioned the accuracy of sniffer dogs. There, Justice Souter wrote, citing reported dog sniffing cases, "The infallible dog, however, is a creature of legal fiction.... Their supposed infallibility is belied by judicial opinions describing well-trained animals sniffing and alerting with less than perfect accuracy, whether owing to errors by their handlers, the limitations of the dogs themselves, or even the pervasive contamination of currency [money] by cocaine."

Justice Deschamps continued:

> Broadly based studies demonstrate an enormous variation in sniffer dog performances, with some dogs giving false positives more than 50 percent of the time. Canadian police data seem not to be available, but in 2006, the [Australian] New South Wales Ombudsman issued a report containing extensive empirical data on the use of sniffer dogs by police since the introduction of the Police Powers Act. During the review period, 17 different drug detection dogs made 10,211 indications during general drug detection operations. The Ombudsman reported:

"Almost all persons indicated by a drug detection dog were subsequently searched by police. This is in accordance with police policy which states that an indication by a drug detection dog gives police reasonable suspicion to search a person.

"Prohibited drugs were only located in 26 percent of the searches following an indication. *That is, almost three-quarters of all indications did not result in the location of prohibited drugs* [emphasis added].

"The rate of finding drugs varied from dog to dog, ranging from 7 percent (of all indications) to 56 percent. (NSW Ombudsman, *Review of the Police Powers (Drug Detections Dogs) Act 2001* (2006), at p. ii.)"

Justice Deschamps added:

Moreover, the sniff does not disclose the presence of drugs. It discloses the presence of an odour that indicates *either* the drugs are present *or* may have been present but are no longer present, or that the dog is simply wrong. Odour attaches to circulating currency and coins. In the sniffer dog business, there are many variables.

I mention these conflicting reports because it is important not to treat the capacity and accuracy of sniffer dogs as interchangeable from one dog to the next. Dogs are not mechanical or chemical devices.

The police claim that they have available dogs like Chief who have a high accuracy rate and a low percentage of false positives. If the lawfulness of a search is challenged, the outcome may depend on evidence before the court in each case about the individual dog and its established reliability. Neither the police nor other government authorities are justified in relying on the "myth of the infallible dog." Proper police manuals require a handler to record a dog's (or the team's) performance. This is (or should be) accepted as an essential part of a handler's work (see S. Bryson, *Police Dog Tactics* (2nd ed. 2000); R. S. Eden, *K9 Officer's Manual* (1993)), to be adduced as part of the evidentiary basis laid before the trial court at which sniffer dog evidence is sought to be introduced.

THE QUEEN v. A.M.: THE FACTS

In 2000, the principal of St. Patrick's High School in Sarnia, Ontario, extended an invitation to the Youth Bureau of Sarnia Police Services: If the police ever had sniffer dogs available to bring into the school to search for drugs, they were welcome to do so.

Apparently, on a few occasions before the case of *The Queen v. A.M.*, police took advantage of the invitation. They used sniffer dogs to check the school parking lot, hallways, and other areas that the principal suggested. The record in this case does not indicate the results of the sniffer checks. However, Sarnia police used sniffer dog searches in at least 140 instances in schools. Further, the use of sniffer dogs in high schools apparently is widely practised in Ontario and other provinces.

The school had a zero-tolerance policy for possession and use of drugs and alcohol, a policy that the school communicated to the students and their parents. Violating this policy resulted in suspension or expulsion of the offending students.

On November 7, 2002, three police officers decided to go to the school with a sniffer dog. The principal granted them permission to go through the school.

At trial, the police officers admitted that they had no information that drugs were then present in the school. The officers acknowledged that they had no grounds to obtain a search warrant. And the principal acknowledged that he had no information about drugs in the school at that time, although he said, "It's pretty safe to assume that they *could* be there."

In cross-examination, the principal was questioned. "But you never, armed with specific information, had called [the police] and said this is what I know, therefore I think a search should be conducted." He answered, "No."

Constable Callander of the Sarnia police gave similar evidence. He was asked: "You did not have any direct awareness as to the existence of drugs and where that might be, and there was no indication that safety of people/students were at risk. You were not armed with any of that kind of information." He answered, "No."

The principal had heard occasional reports from parents or neighbours about "kids in our school who are doing drugs," but nothing specific to the November 7, 2002, time period.

To facilitate the police search, the principal used the school's public address system to tell everyone that the police were on the premises and that students should stay in their classrooms until the police had conducted their search. The effect of this announcement was that no student could leave his or her classroom for the duration of the police investigation.

The police, not the school authorities, took charge of the investigation. The principal testified that he had no involvement beyond giving permission and telling the students to remain in their classrooms. There was no discussion with him as to how the search was to be conducted.

The police search included the gymnasium. A police officer, a canine handler, was accompanied by his sniffer dog, Chief, trained to detect heroin, marijuana, hashish, crack cocaine, and cocaine.

There were no students in the school gymnasium but some backpacks were lying next to the wall. Chief alerted to one of the backpacks by biting at it — as he had been trained to do. The police handler gave the backpack indicated to Constable Callander, who physically searched through its contents.

The constable confirmed Chief's identification of drugs, including five bags of marijuana; a tin box containing a further five bags of marijuana; a bag containing approximately ten magic mushrooms (psilocybin); and a bag containing a pipe, a lighter, rolling papers, and a roach clip. A.M.'s wallet, containing his identification, was in the backpack. A.M. was charged with possession of marijuana for the purpose of trafficking and possession of psilocybin.

FINDINGS OF THE LOWER COURTS

Both the Ontario Youth Justice Court and the Ontario Court of Appeal ruled the searches unreasonable, with the result that the evidence seized was excluded and the charges against A.M. were dismissed. The youth court judge did not find any "bad faith" on the part of the police or the school principal. Still, the youth court judge said that the rights of every student at the school were violated on the day of the search. They were confined to their classroom while the dog sniffed.

In effect, the youth court judge stated that two searches were conducted on the day in question. The first search was the sniffer dog search, which resulted in the dog alerting police to A.M.'s backpack in the school gym. The second was physically searching the questioned backpack, a search that yielded the drugs.

A unanimous Court of Appeal affirmed the youth court judge's decision. To the Court of Appeal, the central questions were:

1. Did the police conduct amount to a search?
2. If so, was the search unreasonable within the meaning of section 8 of the Charter?

(The relevant Charter provisions have been described earlier in "A Standard: The Charter of Rights and Freedoms." Still, it may be useful to repeat the language of section 8: "Everyone has the right to be secure against unreasonable search and seizure.")

CHALLENGE QUESTION

THE ROLE OF SCHOOL AUTHORITIES

Q: Would the search have been unreasonable within section 8 of the Charter had the principal ordered the search — and not the police as in the case of The Queen v. A.M. *— and had the police brought the suspicious backpack to the principal and had the principal turned over its illegal contents to the police?*

A somewhat similar case involving a school-initiated search — *The Queen v. M. (M.R.)*, [1998] 3 *Supreme Court of Canada Reports* 393 — was noted several times in *The Queen v. A.M.* This was an 8-1 decision of the Supreme Court. We will set out the facts and the Court's reasoning and conclusions.

The Queen v. M. (M.R.), in a decision handed down by Justice Peter Cory, allowed a vice-principal to search a thirteen-year-old junior high school student, M.R., in the presence of police. They found a small quantity of marijuana. It was turned over to the police, and M.R. was charged. Several students had earlier informed the vice-principal that M.R. possessed drugs and that he intended to sell them to other students. That night, the school held a dance, for which the vice-principal was responsible.

These were the facts, as stated by Justice Cory:

> When [the vice-principal] saw [the student] arrive at the dance, he called the RCMP to request that an officer attend at the school. He then approached [the student] and his friend and asked them to come to his office. He asked each of the students if they were in possession of drugs and advised them that he was going to search them.
>
> The RCMP officer ... then arrived, dressed in plain clothes. He spoke briefly with [the vice-principal] outside the room, then entered, identified himself to the two boys and sat down. He did not say anything while [the vice-principal] spoke to the students and searched them.
>
> [The student under suspicion] turned out his pockets and, at the request of [the vice-principal], pulled up his pant legs. The vice-principal noticed a bulge in [the student's] sock and removed a cellophane bag. He gave the bag to [the RCMP officer] who identified the contents as marijuana. [The officer] then advised [the student] that he was under arrest for possession of marijuana and read to him the police caution and his right to counsel. [The officer] also advised him that he had the right to contact a parent

or adult. [The student] attempted unsuccessfully to reach his mother by phone and stated that he did not wish to contact anyone else. [The officer] and [the student] then went to [the student's] locker and searched it, but nothing was found there.

At trial, the judge concluded that the search had violated [the student's] rights under the Charter and excluded the evidence found in the search. The Crown did not offer any further evidence, and the charge against [the student] was dismissed. The Court of Appeal allowed the Crown's appeal and ordered a new trial. Thereafter, leave to appeal to this Court (the Supreme Court of Canada) was granted.

For the Court, Justice Cory stated:

- The vice-principal conducted the search. The police constable had no role in this regard. He was passive.
- The vice-principal had reasonable grounds for suspicion that the student had drugs. The student informants had given reliable information in the past.
- The school had a clear policy against unlawful drugs on the premises.
- The school administrators, including the vice-principal as well as the teachers, were mandated by law to ensure good order, discipline, and safety of students.

- Students had to understand that their rights to privacy had to be confined within the limits of what it takes to run an orderly and safe school.
- The search was reasonable and respectful of the student. It took place within the vice-principal's office. The principal gave the student the opportunity to produce the unlawful drugs.
- Justice Cory indicated that if the police officer had conducted the search, the Court may have applied a different and higher standard.

The case of *The Queen v. M. (M.R.)* was different from *The Queen v. A.M.*, where the police initiated and carried out the search. The principal was merely there at the bidding of the police. Further, and perhaps more importantly, in *The Queen v. A.M.* there was, on the facts, no reasonable basis for believing that any student had on his/her person unlawful drugs. At most, the principal suspected that he might find such drugs.

On the facts in this challenge question, the search would likely be deemed unlawful because there was no basis for a reasonable suspicion that students had carried unlawful drugs into the school. Even with a lower standard for school administrators for conducting a search, the administration must have a reasonable basis for suspicion that unlawful drugs are present.

THE QUEEN v. A.M.:
THE SUPREME COURT OF CANADA DECIDES

The Supreme Court of Canada consists of nine justices. A majority (five justices) is enough to constitute a decision binding on the lower courts. In the case of *The Queen v. A.M.*, the Court's decision was fragmented: parts of it brought majority holdings and parts of it brought no majority. To the extent there was no majority ruling, the issues there reflected are not settled. (Of course, if only eight justices took part in a decision, and they split 4–4, then the decision of the lower court would remain in effect. At times, the Court will decide cases in panels of seven justices. Then a majority consists of four justices.)

We will begin with two issues that the Court majority did resolve:

1. Does section 8 of the Charter protect students while in school?
2. Was there a search within the meaning of section 8 of the Charter?

Seven justices ruled that there was such a search and, in that regard, that students were protected by section 8 of the Charter. Justice LeBel stated this, speaking for himself and Justices Morris Fish, Abella, and Charron, and reflecting the conclusions as to this aspect of the case in the concurring opinion of Justice Binnie and Chief Justice McLachlin.

(Note that Justice Bastarache also agreed that there was a search, and that it was one that violated section 8 of the Charter. However, as we pointed out elsewhere, he would have allowed the evidence to be admitted at the trial of A.M. Justices Deschamps and Rothstein dissented from the majority view. They argued that A.M. could not claim rights under section 8 of the Charter because, on the facts, he had no reasonable expectation of privacy, a condition necessary for applying section 8 of the Charter. See, "Dissent from the Majority: A Lawful Search," in this chapter.)

Justice LeBel stated:

> I have read the reasons of my colleague Binnie J. I agree that the appeal should be dismissed.... Students are entitled to privacy even in a school environment.... Entering a schoolyard does not amount to crossing the border of a foreign state. Students ought to be able to attend school without undue interference from the state, but subject, always, to normal school discipline.
>
> As found by the Court of Appeal and by Binnie J., a search was conducted. The authority for that search was nowhere to be found in the statute law or at common law. This is not a case, for example, where the police would have entered the school under the authority of a search warrant and used sniffer dogs to assist in effecting a more focused search. Nor was the dog-sniffer search conducted by the school authorities on proper grounds as set out in *M. (M.R.)*. [Discussed in "Challenge Question: The Role of School Authorities."]
>
> Our Court should not attempt to craft a legal framework of general application for the use of sniffer dogs in schools. As a result, the evidence was properly excluded under section 24(2) of the Canadian Charter of Rights and Freedoms. I would dismiss the appeal.

(See "You Be the Judge: Bus Station Stakeout." The reasoning in the case discussed in the exercise was incorporated into the reasoning of Justice LeBel.)

WHAT KIND OF SEARCH?

In effect, the Court majority found no reasonable basis for a suspicion of wrongdoing that would have legitimized the search under section 8 of the Charter:

> If there were grounds for *reasonable suspicion* that an unlawful act had been committed, or, in this case, that a student had been or was trafficking in prohibited drugs, a search by a sniffer dog likely would have been permitted. But, even in reaching this conclusion, it would be necessary to ask — *what kind of search?* Here the search did not involve the students, as such. That is, they were not forced to a physical search. Indeed, they were not even in the area where the search was conducted [emphasis added].

The concurring opinion of Justice Binnie and Chief Justice McLachlin was:

> If the sniff is conducted on the basis of *reasonable suspicion* [emphasis added] and discloses the presence of illegal drugs on the person or in a backpack or other place of concealment, the police may, in my view, confirm the accuracy of that information with a physical search, again without prior judicial authorization.... But, of course, all such searches by the dogs or the police are subject to after-the-fact judicial review if it is alleged (as here) that no grounds of reasonable suspicion existed, or that the search was otherwise carried out in an unreasonable manner.
>
> Here the after-the-fact judicial review [resulted] when the prosecution attempted to

rely on the evidence obtained in the search. The exceptional authority given to the police to use sniffer dogs on the basis of reasonable suspicion and without prior judicial authorization will, if abused, lead to important consequences under section 24(2) of the Charter which provides that where a court concludes ... "that evidence was obtained in a manner that infringed or denied any rights or freedoms guaranteed by this Charter, the evidence shall be excluded (from consideration) if it is established that, having regard to all the circumstances, the admission of it in the proceedings would bring the administration of justice into disrepute." [See "You Be The Judge: The Scales of Justice" in this chapter.]

The exclusion (of the evidence from consideration) remedy was granted in this case and, in my opinion, rightly so.

I accept the youth court judge's finding of fact that this was a *random speculative search* [emphasis added]. What was done here may have been seen by the police as an efficient use of their resources, and by the principal of the school as an efficient way to advance a zero-tolerance policy. But these objectives were achieved at the expense of the privacy interest (and constitutional rights) of every student in the school, as the youth court judge and the Court of Appeal pointed out. The Charter weighs other values, including privacy, against an appetite for police efficiency. A hunch is not enough to warrant a search of citizens or their belongings by police dogs.

PRIVACY: A PROTECTED INTEREST

Justice Binnie and the chief justice said that section 8 of the Charter is designed to protect the *privacy* interests of individuals. And, again, this interest includes students. They wrote:

> Section 8, like the rest of the Charter, must be interpreted purposively, that is to say, to further the interests it was intended to protect. While these interests may go beyond privacy, they go at least that far.... A privacy interest worthy of protection is one the citizen subjectively believes ought to be respected by the government and that society is prepared to recognize as reasonable.... In each case, an assessment must be made as to whether in a particular situation the public's interest in being left alone by government must give way to the government's interest in intruding on the individual's privacy in order to advance its goals, notably those of law enforcement.

These are the considerations that brought the Court to this conclusion:

- "The restraints imposed on government to pry into the lives of the citizen go to the essence of a democratic state.... Students are as deserving of constitutional protection as adults — although their age, vulnerability, and presence in a school environment all factor into the totality of the circumstances."
- The Court's "focus must be on the impact on the subject of the search or the seizure [here, all the students at the school], and not simply on its rationality in furthering some valid government objective. The impact includes disruption, inconvenience and potential embarrass-

ment for innocent individuals subjected to the dog sniff or other intrusive police attention."

- Obviously, the Court must know the purpose of the police search in determining its validity. "If the police in this case had been called to investigate the potential presence of guns or explosives at the school using dogs trained for that purpose, the public interest in dealing quickly and efficiently with such a threat to public safety, even if speculative, would have been greater and more urgent than routine crime prevention. Generally speaking, the legal balance would have come down on the side of the use of sniffer dogs to get to the bottom of a possible threat to the lives or immediate safety and well-being of the students and staff."

- "The Court must consider the significance of the information obtained as a result of the [search]. Of course, much police work does consist of assembling different 'scraps' of information, some of it apparently meaningless, into a significant picture. This fact does not necessarily generate constitutional protection for the 'meaningless scraps' that form part of the mosaic unless there is something else in the context that drives that result. In the present case, [this consideration] is inapplicable. The information [here] is highly meaningful. We are not dealing with 'scraps.' The dogs pointed the police to the sniffer dog's equivalent of a smoking gun."

- Finally, the courts "have to deal with what is presented to them as reality." It is true that a sniffer dog may alert police to information about the crime under investigation. And, having said this, the Court made it clear that the subject of such investigatory tools is not finally resolved by this case. Other facts may bring other results.

APPLYING FACTS

Justice Binnie and the chief justice applied the following principles to the arguments that the Crown raised:

- It is true that the students knew that the school setting was closely supervised and regulated. Indeed, A.M.'s school principal had made clear the board of education and school policy of zero-tolerance of unlawful drugs.

In carrying forward that policy, wasn't it logical to allow sniffer dog police searches? Isn't this a legitimate incursion on the rights of students? The answer from Justice Binnie and the chief justice was this: There was a general expectation of privacy that did not end because of a generalized fear of drugs. The threat had to be more immediate; it had to be based on a real suspicion.

- Yet doesn't A.M. in effect ask that his privacy interest be one of protecting "contraband"? The dog's sniff relates only to illegal drugs. Justice Binnie and the chief justice quoted with approval a dissent of then U.S. Supreme Court Justice Brennan when faced with a similar prosecution argument:

> Under the Court's analysis in these cases, law enforcement officers could release a trained cocaine-sensitive dog — to paraphrase the California Court of Appeal, a "canine cocaine connoisseur" — to roam the streets at random, alerting the officers to people carrying cocaine.... Or, if a device were developed that, when aimed at a person, would detect instantaneously whether the person is carrying cocaine, there would be no Fourth Amendment [U.S. Constitution] bar [against unlawful search and

seizure — similar to section 8 of the Charter], under the Court's approach, to the police setting up such a device on a street corner and scanning all passersby.

In fact, the Court's analysis is so unbounded that if a device were developed that could detect, from the outside of a building, the presence of cocaine inside, there would be no constitutional obstacle to the police cruising through a residential neighborhood and using the device to identify all homes in which the drug is present. In short, under the interpretation of the Fourth Amendment ... first applied in this case, these surveillance techniques would not constitute searches and therefore could be freely pursued whenever and wherever law enforcement officers desire. Hence, at some point in the future, if the Court stands by the theory it has adopted today, search warrants, probable cause, and even "reasonable suspicion" may very well become notions of the past.

The means, said Justice Binnie and the chief justice, do not justify the end. The focus of any search must be on the person, place, or thing searched. A suspicionless search should not be rendered acceptable by after-the-fact discovery of unlawful drugs. Justice Binnie wrote for himself and the chief justice:

I therefore do not agree with the Crown's argument that A.M.'s reasonable privacy interest in the contents of his backpack extended only to what was lawful and excluded what was unlawful. On the contrary, I expect A.M. would not have cared if the police had found a polished apple for the

teacher in his backpack. He would very much
care about discovery of illicit drugs. In past cases,
we have accepted a legitimate privacy interest in
a home despite the presence therein of drug[s]
(*The Queen v. Evans*, [1996] 1 *Supreme Court of
Canada Reports* 8) ... and an automobile despite
the discovery of incriminating evidence (*The
Queen v. Mellenthin*, [1992] 3 *Supreme Court of
Canada Reports* 615)....There is no reason why a
student's privacy interest in his backpack should
not be deemed similarly respected despite the
presence of contraband.

- An argument could be made that the police dog was
  merely sniffing air, something that all of us breathe.
  It was an action that everyone does. How can it be
  said that such action was a search? Justice Binnie and
  the chief justice seemed to reject the argument out-of-
  hand. Justice Binnie stated:

  Dogs have a capacity not available to human
  beings. The better analogy is to a machine or device
  for detecting odours (such as a smoke alarm),
  although dogs, being living creatures, are more
  variable than machines in their performance.

  The dog "sniffing" cannot be treated as an isolated phenomenon and detached from the broader
  police conduct. I do not think it is plausible for the
  Crown to argue at one and the same time that the
  sniffer-dog utility lies in quick accurate identification of illicit drugs concealed inside a backpack,
  but that the result is not a search.

THE IMPORTANCE OF FACTS

Justice Binnie and Chief Justice McLachlin were trying to develop guidelines that the Court could apply in any case. But the nature of the problem of investigative devices applied to crime is a rapidly developing field. The technology of today may be replaced by another technology tomorrow.

Justice Binnie and the chief justice emphasized the need to be open to review any new technology in the context of section 8 of the Charter. They acknowledged, for example, the potential use of honeybees and sensors to scan crowds on the lookout for possible wrongdoing (Kerr and McGill 2007, cited by Justice Binnie).

Justice Binnie wrote,

> The [Charter's] section 8 jurisprudence will continue to evolve as snooping technology advances. This flexibility is essentially what the totality of the circumstances approach is designed to achieve. On these occasions, critics usually refer to "Orwellian dimensions" and *1984* [a famous book by George Orwell suggesting a future where privacy would be a right long gone], but the fact is that *1984* came and went without George Orwell's fears being entirely realized, although he saw earlier than most the direction in which things might be heading. The Court can insist on proper evidence of what the police or government are up to and how, if at all, the information the police seek to collect can be used.... Whatever evolution occurs in the future will have to be dealt with by the courts step by step. Concerns should be addressed with as they truly arise.

YOU BE THE JUDGE

THE SCALES OF JUSTICE

THE FACTS

The facts are taken from *The Queen v. A.M.* In effect, a high school was locked down. Students were ordered to stay in their classrooms for a period of about two hours while police, at the invitation of the school principal, conducted a sniffer dog search for unlawful drugs.

The dog sniffed such drugs — and alerted police — in the school gym where a number of students had placed their backpacks. The police opened the backpack in question and found and seized marijuana and "magic" mushrooms. The identity of the student owner of the backpack was determined and he was charged.

The youth court determined, and the Supreme Court of Canada agreed, that the search was unlawful within the meaning of the Charter of Rights and Freedoms. However, the Crown argued that, in any event, the evidence resulting from that search should be allowed at trial.

THE ISSUES

Under what circumstances, if any, may unlawfully seized evidence be presented by the Crown in a criminal trial? Who is in the best position to make that decision?

POINTS TO CONSIDER

- The Charter of Rights and Freedoms is part of the Constitution of Canada and, as such, it is the highest law of the land.
- Section 24(2) of the Charter allows a court to hear evidence from unlawful searches that would otherwise be excluded in a criminal trial. But this can be done only if such admission would not "bring the administration of justice into disrepute."
- These are the relevant provisions of the Charter:

  24(1) Anyone whose rights or freedoms, as guaranteed by this Charter, have been infringed or denied may apply to a court of competent jurisdiction to obtain such remedy as the court considers appropriate and just in the circumstances.

  24(2) Where, in proceedings under sub-section (1), a court concludes that evidence was obtained in a manner that infringed or denied any rights or freedoms guaranteed by this Charter, the evidence shall be excluded if it is established that, having regard to all the circumstances, the admission of it in the proceedings would bring the administration of justice into disrepute.

- The Ontario Education Act calls for police to be used only "when necessary, or if the well-being of the student is at risk."
- Drug use and trafficking among and by youth is considered a serious societal problem.

DISCUSSION

The Court majority in *The Queen v. A.M.*, having ruled the sniff search unlawful, sustained the trial court refusal to receive the results of that search (the unlawful drugs) in evidence. Justice Binnie, with whom Chief Justice McLachlin concurred, stated that (1) drugs in schools are a serious problem, but (2) the trial court judge (youth court) saw the parties and heard the evidence. That judge was in a better position to balance the rights of A.M. against those of the need to protect society.

Justice Binnie noted that the trial court's decision should be upheld on appeal unless it was based on a wrong principle or exercised in an unreasonable manner. The trial court is seen as reflecting community values.

Justice Binnie then went on to quote the youth court judge who stated:

> This search was unreasonable from the outset. It is completely contrary to the requirements of the law with respect to the search in a school setting. To admit the evidence is effectively to strip A.M. and any other student in a similar situation of the right to be free from unreasonable search and seizure. It is effectively saying

that persons in the same situation as A.M.
have no rights. Such a finding would, to
my mind, bring the administration of justice into disrepute.

CREATING A BALANCE
At this point, Justice Binnie reviewed the findings of the
youth court judge:

> The evidence was essential to the Crown's
> case. Without it, the case could be and
> was dismissed. Further, having regard to
> the school setting, the youth court judge
> said, "the breach must be seen on the less
> serious end of the scale." Involved was no
> crime of violence, and the drugs involved
> might be seen as less pernicious than
> those such as cocaine or heroin. No bad
> faith could be attributed to the police or
> school authorities. All of these factors,
> said the youth court judge, tended to
> favour admission of the evidence despite
> the Charter breaches.
>
> However, the youth court judge con-
> tinued, weighed against admission was
> the fact that the use of dogs for a "gen-
> eral sweep" in this case appears to be the
> standard practice of the OPP [Ontario
> Provincial Police] and the municipal
> police forces in Ontario. The searches did
> not respect the rules set out four years
> previously by this Court in *The Queen v.*

M. (M.R.). Nor did they comply with the school board's own policies enacted under the Ontario Education Act, which call for police to be used only "when necessary, or if the well-being of the student is at risk." The police in this matter acknowledged that they had participated in sniffer dog searches of schools on approximately 140 previous occasions.

The failure to respect the right of the students may therefore be described as systemic — that is, reflective of the way the system, as a whole, operated. In the end, weighing the good with the bad, the youth court judge concluded that "the Charter must not be seen as something to be swept away in the interests of expediency. While this case centres around the rights of A.M., the rights of every student in the school were violated that day as they were all subject to an unreasonable search."

Justice Binnie concluded:

Like the Ontario Court of Appeal, I would not interfere with the balance of competing values struck by the youth court judge or his exclusion of the evidence. Youth court judges carry out special responsibilities for young people in trouble with the law. They have a greater awareness than appellate judges do of the effect that admission or exclusion of this evidence would have on the reputation of the administration of justice in the community with which they deal on a daily basis. The trial judge's analysis was brief but perceptive. I would not interfere.

A DISSENTING VIEW

Justice Bastarache agreed with the Court majority that the sniffer search was unlawful. He dissented, however, on the application of section 24(2) of the Charter. He would have allowed the evidence resulting from the unlawful search to be received. It seemed to him that (1) trafficking in prohibited drugs was a serious matter in itself. An aggravating factor was that the offence took place within a school. (2) The principal and police conducted the search in the good faith belief that they were acting in a lawful manner. To Justice Bastarache, the illegality of the search was inadvertent.

Justice Bastarache stated:

> Although this search was not performed on the basis of a reasonable suspicion that drugs would be found, it was conducted in good faith. The search was non-intrusive in nature [for example, none of the students were subject to a physical search] and occurred in an environment where the [personal] expectation of privacy was diminished. The evidence obtained was non-conscriptive [obtained not by force but found in a student's stored backpack]

in nature and does not affect the fairness of the trial. As a result, it is my view that excluding this evidence would bring the administration of justice into disrepute and that the trial judge erred by failing to admit it at trial.

DISSENT FROM THE MAJORITY: A LAWFUL SEARCH

Justices Deschamps and Rothstein dissented from the majority view. They argued that A.M. could not claim rights under section 8 of the Charter because, on the facts, he had no reasonable expectation of privacy — a condition necessary for applying section 8 of the Charter.

To the dissenting justices, the question was not whether there was a search by the sniffer police dog. The Crown had argued, among other points, that the dog was simply sniffing air. It had not physically forced open, nor in any way impinged on, any backpack.

Justice Deschamps stated:

A.M.'s backpack was closed and was in a pile with others in the small gymnasium of St. Patrick's High School when the police officers entered the room with their sniffer dog. It is significant that the odours emanating from the backpack could not be detected by the police using their own senses and that the police necessarily relied on the use of the dog to identify, among the several backpacks in the gymnasium, which, if any, contained controlled substances.

The dog's positive indication on sniffing A.M.'s backpack enabled the police to ascertain what was *inside* the backpack with a reasonably high degree of accuracy. Accordingly, I have no difficulty in finding that the use of the dog in this case amounted to a search from an *empirical* perspective. However, what A.M. had to establish was that the use of the dog amounted to a "search" from a constitutional perspective such that it implicated a reasonable expectation of privacy that engaged the protection of section 8.

A REASONABLE EXPECTATION OF PRIVACY

Justice Deschamps emphasized that A.M. was not wearing the backpack at the time of the search. It was in a pile of other student backpacks. It would be a different case, she said, if A.M. had been wearing the backpack at the time of the search. Still, the question remained as to whether A.M. had a reasonable expectation of privacy — that his backpack would be left alone.

For the dissent, Justice Deschamps argued that A.M. had neither a subjective nor objective reasonable expectation of privacy. The justice wrote:

> Students and parents were aware of the drug problem and the school's zero-tolerance drug policy and of the fact that sniffer dogs might be used. Dogs had in fact been used on prior occasions to determine whether narcotics were present at the school....

Nor can it be said, Justice Deschamps continued, that A.M. could have had any objective expectation of privacy. She wrote:

> The place where the search occurred was a school with a known problem of drug use by students, both on and off school property....
>
> The police were there with the permission (and at the request) of the school's principal in furtherance of disciplinary goals being pursued by the school in order to confront a systematic drug problem. The dogs were used to search the premises, not the students....

Justice Deschamps added:

> The use of a sniffer dog as an investigative technique did not intrude unreasonably on A.M.'s privacy interest, since his informational privacy interest was extremely limited in the school environment. Therefore, in my view, in light of [all] of the circumstances, A.M. did not have a reasonable expectation of privacy that engaged section 8.
>
> Since I am of the view that A.M. did not have a reasonable expectation of privacy that engaged section 8 of the Charter, it is not necessary to determine whether the search was reasonable.
>
> Furthermore, since A.M. did not have a reasonable expectation of privacy in respect

> of his backpack that was sufficient to engage section 8 of the Charter, and since the police were lawfully present at the school with the principal's permission and were acting [as is] their duty to investigate and prevent crime, no individualized grounds were required for the police to employ their sniffer dog as they did in this case.

THE MEDIA'S RESPONSE

Within hours of the release of the decision in *The Queen v. A.M.*, the *Globe and Mail* featured a lengthy editorial comment, a portion of which follows:

> When a high-school principal in Sarnia, Ont., turned his school over to the police for a good portion of the day to let a drug-sniffing dog roam, he sent a terrible message to his students about what a democracy should permit the state to do in pursuit of its goals. The students were locked in their classrooms for up to two hours while the dog and the police did their work, intruding at random on the students' personal property. For part of the day, that zero-tolerance school must have felt like a police state.
>
> It is good that the Supreme Court of Canada ruled this 2002 search illegal yesterday, and refused to allow evidence of 10 bags of marijuana and 10 magic mushrooms found in a backpack in the [school] gymnasium to be used against

the student who owned it. But, the Court, like Canadians generally, was torn over the appropriate standard for police as they go about their work of detecting crime and protecting communities. To a surprising extent, the Court is at sea....

Charter rights are not guarantees of ideal justice, because they exist in the real world. A random drug search is of small use if the price is to render students rights-less. But holding police to an abstract standard of perfection as they try to protect us against imminent danger would give the Charter a bad name ("At Sea, but Keeping a Balance" 2008).

YOU BE THE JUDGE

BUS STATION STAKEOUT

THE FACTS

On January 25, 2002, at about 11:00 a.m., three RCMP officers in plain clothes were staking out the Calgary Greyhound bus terminal. The team was watching passengers leave the overnight bus from Vancouver.

This was part of the RCMP "Jetway" program, which monitors the travelling public in an effort to identify and arrest drug couriers and other individuals participating in criminal activities. This was the only purpose of the stakeout.

The officers were not investigating the possibility of terrorist activity, explosives, or other threats to public safety. Their sniffer dog, Chevy, was not trained for anything other than narcotics detection.

RCMP Sergeant MacPhee testified that his training in the Jetway program taught him to watch for an "elongated stare," a locked eye contact for a period of a few seconds. One passenger gave him such a stare. Sergeant MacPhee noted that the man had moved to the underbelly of the bus, but did not look at the bags that were being unloaded. Instead, he went around the bus in a direction different from the other passengers and stopped approximately three to five metres behind Sergeant MacPhee. The officer said this conduct aroused his suspicion.

The passenger was carrying a bag (like a gym bag) that had no Greyhound or other identifying tags on it. It had two handles rather than a shoulder strap, and he was carrying it on his shoulder. On entering the terminal, he walked toward the washroom. About five metres before the washroom door, he stopped, turned around and looked back at Sergeant MacPhee, who was about eight metres behind him. Sergeant MacPhee described this as "rubber-necking."

When the passenger came out of the washroom, he again made eye contact with Sergeant MacPhee as he moved toward the exit doors. Sergeant MacPhee went over and introduced himself as follows: "Good morning, sir. I'm a police officer out here at the bus terminal. You're not in any sort of trouble and you're free to go at any time. We just talk to people as they're travelling."

Sergeant MacPhee commented on the weather and asked to see the passenger's bus ticket (which he had apparently left on the bus), and asked for identification (which the man produced). Sergeant MacPhee made a note of his name and date of birth, and asked how long he would be in Calgary. The passenger seemed to Sergeant MacPhee to be getting "increasingly antsy" in the officer's presence.

At this point, Sergeant MacPhee asked to see the contents of the passenger's bag. The man paused, then put his bag down on the floor and started to open it. Sergeant MacPhee said, "Thanks, sir. You're certainly not obliged to show me, but thanks."

Sergeant MacPhee then started to kneel down and take hold of the bag himself, saying: "Just an officer safety thing here, do you mind?" Before he could touch the bag, the passenger said "What are you doing?" and pulled the bag back.

At that point, the passenger was very agitated. Sergeant MacPhee signalled to another officer, Sergeant (then Corporal) Bouey, who was accompanied by Chevy, a police sniffer dog, as noted. They approached, and Chevy sat down, indicating to his handler the presence of drugs in the bag. Sergeant MacPhee then told the passenger that he was under arrest for the possession and/or trafficking of a controlled substance and advised him of his rights.

Following the arrest, the passenger's bag was searched by Constable Ritchie, and was found to contain two zip lock baggies filled with approximately half a kilogram of cocaine. The accused also produced, from his pocket, a Starbucks mint container containing a small amount of heroin. He was charged with possession of cocaine for the purposes of trafficking and possession of heroin.

The trial judge ruled that the accused was neither arbitrarily detained nor unlawfully searched, and he entered a conviction. The majority of the Court of Appeal agreed and dismissed his appeal.

THE ISSUE

Was there a lawful basis for police search of the accused's luggage?

POINTS TO CONSIDER

- Section 8 of the Charter of Rights and Freedoms, part of the Constitution of Canada, provides, "Everyone has the right to be secure against unreasonable search or seizure."
- Based on the reasoning of the Supreme Court of Canada in *The Queen v. A.M.*, the sniffer dog's alert in front of the luggage of the accused was a search.
- The offences with which the accused was charged were serious. However, if the search were unlawful, the breach of his section 8 Charter rights also would have been serious.
- The accused had a "reasonable expectation of privacy" in the luggage that he carried, which was protected by the Charter.
- There is no statute that defines authority for a lawful canine search.

DISCUSSION

The facts in this case were taken from *The Queen v. Kang-Brown*, a decision handed down by the Supreme Court of Canada on the same day as *The Queen v. A.M.* The Court reflected the same split as in *The Queen v. A.M.* A majority of the Court agreed with the conclusion that the sniff and the luggage search were unlawful and that the seriousness of the breach of section 8 of the Charter required that the evidence arising from the search should be excluded under section 24(2) of the Charter.

IMPORTANT DIFFERENCES

There were, however, important differences between the two cases. In *The Queen v. A.M.*, the search took place in a high school. This setting, Justice LeBel emphasized, requires different criteria, a different standard for measuring the lawfulness of searches. Educational institutions, such as high schools, have a duty to care for the security and well-being of students. This duty is made explicit by statute. The difficulty with the search in *The Queen v. A.M.* was that the search was initiated and conducted by the police, who simply took advantage of an earlier general invitation from the school principal.

A different result might have ensued (1) if the principal had received more specific and current information of drug trafficking in the school close to the time the search was made, and (2) if the principal had ordered and/or conducted the search — even in the presence of the police as backup. If these conditions had been met, then the standard for measuring the lawfulness of the search would have been reasonable suspicion of unlawful drug trafficking. (3) Further, if there were a threat of violence (guns, explosives), the police would have been able to conduct a search, even without the permission of a principal. On the facts in both cases, there was no use of sniffer dogs to alert for explosives. The dogs were trained only to alert for certain drugs.

In *The Queen v. Kang-Brown*, the search and the arrest that followed took place in a bus depot. Justice LeBel, for himself and Justices Fish, Abella, and Charron, said the higher standard for conducting a search, namely, reasonable and probable cause, should have been used. It was on the legal standard for conducting a search that Justice LeBel and his three colleagues differed with Justice Binnie and the chief justice, who formed the basic majority for the Court's conclusion. To this extent, then, it can be said that there was no Court majority as to the legal standard to be applied in searches in non-school areas.

Our discussion here centres on the opinion of Justice LeBel, who spoke for the largest grouping of the Justices, though they did not constitute a majority of the Court.

Justice LeBel stated:

> Of critical importance in situating the debate before this Court is the undisputed fact that the police had no reasonable and probable grounds to believe that Mr. Kang-Brown had drugs in his possession or that he had committed any other offence at the time they accosted him and effected the sniffer-dog search. The Crown seeks to rely, rather, on the *fruits* of the sniffer-dog search itself to establish the legality of Mr. Kang-Brown's arrest and consequent search of his bag. In other words, it is uncontested that on the present state of the law, without the benefit of the positive sniffer-dog search, Mr. Kang-Brown ought to have been left alone by state authorities.
>
> It is common ground that no statutory provision authorizes the sniffer-dog

search that was conducted at the Calgary bus terminal. Nor was there common law authority to arrest Mr. Kang-Brown prior to the search being conducted....

Contrary to what Binnie J. asserts in his reasons, the issue of the role of the courts in respect of common law police powers is squarely before us on this appeal. Unlike him, however, I conclude that any perceived gap in the present state of the law on police investigative powers arising from the use of sniffer dogs is a matter better left for Parliament. The issue was raised by the parties in this Court and in the courts below. Indeed, it lies at the heart of the present litigation. Mr. Kang-Brown raised the arbitrariness of the search....

Section 8 of the Charter expresses one of the core values of our society: respect for personal privacy and autonomy. A significant proportion of Charter decisions have concerned the interpretation and application of section 8.... Although the word "privacy" does not appear in the Charter, from the first days of its application, section 8 evolved into a shield against unjustified state intrusions on personal privacy....

My concern is that the approach adopted by my colleagues in this case will in practice jeopardize critical elements of the constitutional rights guaranteed by section 8 and of that section's underlying values. Perhaps somewhat ironically, this erosion process would derive not from state action or from the laws of Parliament, but from decisions of the courts themselves.

PARLIAMENT'S ROLE AND THE COURT'S BOUNDARIES

Suppose Parliament enacted a law specifically allowing police to use sniffer dog alerts for unlawful drugs at public commuting terminals. Under the law, police, on an alert, would be permitted to search both a person and his or her luggage. If unlawful drugs were found, the law would permit the Crown to introduce the drugs in evidence in support of charges. How would a court determine the constitutionality of such a law under the Charter?

The key question goes to the justification of the law as a reasonable limit that can be justified in a free and democratic society — as set out in section 1 of the Charter. Justice LeBel, speaking for himself and three other justices in *The Queen v. Kang-Brown*, emphasized that such Parliamentary action gives the Crown the chance to put the reasoning, the facts, and the need for such a law as a reasonable limit on privacy to the Court. He wrote:

> A statutory provision on the appropriate use of sniffer dogs in law enforcement ... might require justification under section 1 [of the Charter], but state action would not be foreclosed so long as the standard for justification was met under the relevant constitutional test. A requirement that Parliament act first would put the courts in a better position to address the competing interests at play and would

ensure that the justification process meets constitutional standards. The extension of common law police powers as proposed in this case would shortcut the justification process and leave the Court to frame the common law rule itself without the full benefit of the dialogue and discussion that would have taken place had Parliament acted and been required to justify its action.

Moreover, this is a case where the courts are ill-equipped to develop an adequate legal framework for the use of police dogs. In determining where the proper balance lies between the protection of privacy and effective law enforcement, the courts will be hampered by the fact that little is known about investigative techniques using sniffer dogs. Indeed, the record remains singularly bereft of useful information about sniffer dogs. The available information is in essence limited to the facts that they are used for investigative purposes in a variety of circumstances and that police officers believe in their overall reliability and to the praise of a particular dog deployed at the Calgary bus station. From the record, however, and from some of the authorities cited by the parties, it appears that serious doubt has occasionally been cast on the reliability of sniffer dogs.... Despite this inadequate record, this Court is nonetheless being asked to curtail Charter rights for fear of leaving a void in the law and interfering with the use of a fairly widespread police investigative technique. The Court would create a new common law rule on the basis of little more than unverified and, for us in this appeal, unverifiable assumptions.

Courts ought to avoid relying on such a weak and inadequate record as a basis for justifying an intrusion on privacy rights. A downgrading of the standard of reasonable and probable cause to a standard of reasonable suspicion in these circumstances and on the basis of this record might lead to an even looser test of "generalized suspicion," which is in fact the standard adopted by one of the dissenting judges in this appeal. It would also tend to limit privacy rights to the possibility of obtaining some kind of remedy after the fact. Perfunctory excuses would be of little comfort to passengers and passers-by inconvenienced by an unfounded sniff and its consequences. The result would verge on honouring reasonable and probable cause in principle, while gutting it in practice through an even wider use of a standard of reasonable suspicion.

The constitution of Canada, including the Charter, is fundamental to our life in this country. The Court needs to have facts that are clear so that constitutional questions can be developed, argued, and decided in ways that will give a certain precedent to the decisions.

REFERENCES AND FURTHER READING
* Cited by the Supreme Court of Canada.

Amsterdam, Anthony G. 1973–74. "Perspectives on the Fourth Amendment." *Minnesota Law Review* 58: 349–477.*

"At Sea, but Keeping a Balance." 2008. *Globe and Mail*, April 26.

Australia. New South Wales. 2006. *Review of the Police Powers (Drug Detections Dogs) Act 2001*. Sydney: New South Wales Ombudsman.*

Australia. New South Wales. 2004. *Discussion Paper: Review of the Police Powers (Drug Detections Dogs) Act.* Sydney: New South Wales Ombudsman.*

Bird, Robert. 1996–97. "An Examination of the Training and Reliability of the Narcotics Detection Dog." *Kentucky Law Journal* 85: 405–33.*

Brennan, Richard. 2008. "Random Searches Curbed." *Toronto Star,* April 26.

Bryson, Sandy. 2000. *Police Dog Tactics.* 2nd ed. Calgary: Detselig Enterprises.*

Davis-Barron, Sherri. 2007. "The Lawful Use of Drug Detector Dogs." *Criminal Law Quarterly* 52: 345–91.*

Eden, Robert S. 1993. *K9 Officer's Manual.* Calgary: Detselig Enterprises.

Katz, Lewis R. 1989–90. "In Search of a Fourth Amendment for the Twenty-First Century." *Indiana Law Journal* 65, no.3: 549–90.*

Katz, Lewis R., and Aaron P. Golembiewski. 2006–7. "Curbing the Dog: Extending the Protection of the Fourth Amendment to Police Drug Dogs." *Nebraska Law Review* 85: 735–92.*

Kerr, Ian, and Jena McGill. 2007. "Emanations, Snoop Dogs and Reasonable Expectations of Privacy." *Criminal Law Quarterly* 52, no.3: 392–432.*

LaFave, Wayne R. 2004. *Search and Seizure: A Treatise on the Fourth Amendment.* 4th ed. Vols. 1 and 4. St. Paul, MN: Thomson/West.*

Lammers, Ken. 2005. "Canine Sniffs: The Search That Isn't." *New York University Journal of Law and Liberty* 1, no. 2: 845–56.*

Makin, Kirk. 2008. "Top Court Puts Leash on Random Searches by Sniffer Dogs." *Globe and Mail,* April 26.

Meehan, Eugene. 2008. "The Supreme Court Defines Man's Best Friend." *National Post,* April 26.

Naumetz, Tim. 2008. "SCC Muzzles Random Police Dog-sniff Searches." *Law Times,* May 5.

Ontario Ministry of Education. 2001. *Ontario Schools: Code of Conduct*. Toronto: Queen's Printer.*

Pollack, Kenneth L. 1994. "Stretching the Terry Doctrine to the Search for Evidence of Crime: Canine Sniffs, State Constitutions, and the Reasonable Suspicion Standard." *Vanderbilt Law Review* 47: 803–55.*

"Random Use of Police Sniffer Dogs Breaches Charter: Top Court." 2008. *CBC.ca*, April 25.

Shaw, Trevor. 2004. "The Law on the Use of Police Dogs in Canada." *Criminal Law Quarterly* 48: 337–66.*

CHAPTER 5
YOUTH: POLICE AND THE RIGHT TO BE WARNED

Police are often an individual's first point of contact with the criminal process. They investigate possible criminal violations and they can detain, arrest, and lay charges against those believed to have violated the criminal law. Police can be seen as the community's first formal agency in bringing the accused to the "dock" — or not.

Here we will discuss those special rules binding on police in dealing with the young. For the most part, the rules for police conduct or interface with the young are set out in the Youth Criminal Justice Act (YCJA), portions of which were set out in previous chapters.

The rules of conduct for police under the YCJA are mandatory. If they fail to follow the rules, the Crown prosecutor may find the case against the accused significantly weakened because the court might throw out evidence derived through improper police procedures. The YCJA, in its interpretation and enforcement, must conform to the Charter of Rights and Freedoms, which as we noted in previous chapters, is part of the Constitution of Canada.

Among the questions raised in this chapter are:

- Can youths be singled out to receive greater rights than adults?

- Are police required to ensure that youths understand any cautions given?
- What results from police failure to give lawful cautions to youths?

There is a protective shield for youths between the ages of twelve and eighteen at the point when they are detained or arrested by police. That shield gives young people greater rights than adults may claim under similar circumstances. Much of this chapter deals with the scope of such rights for youths.

Before going to the sources of youth procedural rights, we will describe the reasons underlying their establishment, as given by the Supreme Court of Canada in the principal case discussed in this chapter: *L.T.H. v. The Queen*, 2008 *Supreme Court of Canada Reports* 49.

Justice Fish spoke for the seven-member Court majority in *L.T.H. v. The Queen*. This is how he began his opinion:

> Young persons, even more than adults, are inclined to feel vulnerable when questioned by police officers who suspect them of crime and can influence their fate. Parliament has for that reason provided them by statute with a complementary set of enhanced procedural safeguards in section 146 of the Youth Criminal Justice Act, Statutes of Canada 2002, chapter 1 (YCJA), which governs the admissibility of statements made to persons in authority by young persons who are accused of committing offences.

These rights, as we shall see, apply to all young persons between the ages of twelve and eighteen. They are cast in terms of procedural rights — such as the right to have counsel and/or an adult present before making a statement to the police. But the failure to

comply with these procedural rights can have real consequences:
The Crown may be denied the right to introduce such statements
in evidence against the accused.

While the intent of the YCJA seems clear — protect vulnerable
youth from police interrogation until they obtain the assistance of
counsel or an adult — a number of questions arose in *L.T.H. v. The
Queen*. They include:

- What must police do to obtain a waiver of a young
  person's right to the assistance of counsel or an adult?
- Will a young person give up the right to counsel or the
  advice of an adult simply by making a clear statement
  to that effect?
- Can police assume that a young person knows his/
  her rights to counsel or assistance of an adult if that
  individual has had frequent contact with the police?
- Does the seriousness of the offence have any bearing
  on whether a trial judge will forgive police errors in
  obtaining a lawful waiver by a young person of the
  right to counsel or the advice of an adult?

To aid in understanding this chapter, we have added section
146 of the YCJA as an appendix.

THE FACTS OF *L.T.H. v. THE QUEEN*

By the time the Supreme Court of Canada handed down its
decision in *L.T.H. v. The Queen*, the accused was nineteen and
no longer a youth within the meaning of the YCJA. The Court
made its decision four years after L.T.H.'s arrest. (This "coming
of age" — of being a young offender at the time of arrest and
moving to adult status at the time of final judgment — often
occurs in YCJA cases.)

L.T.H., then fifteen, was arrested in the early morning hours of August 8, 2004, by the RCMP in Cole Harbour, Nova Scotia, following a car chase that ended only when L.T.H.'s car caught fire and was brought to a stop. Initially, he was charged with dangerous driving. Then, he was transferred to the Halifax Regional Police Service where the charges against him increased. They included theft, possession of property obtained by crime, and failing to stop — as well as the original charge, dangerous driving.

L.T.H. was taken into custody by police at about 5:00 a.m. He was asked several times if he wanted the services of a lawyer. Each time, he refused such assistance.

Several hours after the arrest, police took L.T.H. from the Cole Harbour police station to the Dartmouth police station, where he slept for a few hours. Police then transferred him to the Halifax police station, where Constable Jeffrey Carlisle interviewed him. The constable had a young offender police statement form that he reviewed with L.T.H.

The interview was videotaped, and the Crown made the tape available to the trial court judge, the appellate court, and with the consent of Crown counsel and L.T.H.'s lawyer, to the Supreme Court of Canada, which reviewed it in the appeal that gave rise to the Court's decision.

THE INTERVIEW AND THE WAIVER

This was not the first time that police had interviewed L.T.H. In the hearing before the trial judge, his mother said she had warned the police, at the time of his arrest, that her son had a learning disability that made understanding the questions put to him difficult. In earlier encounters with the police, she said, she had to explain the questions and their meaning to her son.

However, Constable Carlisle pressed on with the interview of L.T.H. He read from questions in the form that included a statement of an accused young offender's rights. He asked L.T.H. if he understood his rights. L.T.H. answered, "Yes." The constable asked L.T.H. if he wanted to call a lawyer or talk with a lawyer in private. L.T.H. answered, "No." L.T.H. also answered that he did not want a parent or "another appropriate adult" present while he gave a statement or while he was questioned.

This is not to say that L.T.H. was frozen in his replies. He did assert himself. At one point, he interrupted Constable Carlisle's reading of the form and said he was "not going to answer all of the questions" asked.

Constable Carlisle responded that the questions were only of the "do-you-understand" type. L.T.H. raised no further objection to the questioning, and Constable Carlisle continued. He finished reading the "waiver-of-rights form," which L.T.H. initialled. L.T.H. then signed a waiver of rights.

At that point, police took a statement from L.T.H. in which he inculpated himself. That is, he confessed to actions that formed the basis of the Crown's case against him.

A TECHNICALITY?

Counsel for L.T.H. challenged the waiver and, with it, the statement that formed the Crown's case against L.T.H. The trial judge agreed. She ruled that the statement could not be received in evidence. The Crown presented no further evidence. The result: The charges against L.T.H. were dismissed. An acquittal was ordered.

The trial judge accepted that L.T.H.'s statement was voluntary. But that was not enough. The trial judge said that the YCJA sets additional requirements for a youth to give a lawful waiver. In this regard, the trial judge said she was not convinced beyond a reasonable doubt that L.T.H. understood his rights and the consequences of waiving them.

The Crown appealed the decision of the trial judge. The Nova Scotia Court of Appeal allowed the appeal. It set aside the acquittal and ordered a new trial. The Court of Appeal ruled that the

Crown must prove beyond a reasonable doubt that the young person was given a clear and proper statement of rights and choices under the YCJA.

But, said the Court of Appeal, the Crown does not have to prove that the young person in fact understood those rights. In this regard, the Court of Appeal acknowledged that actual (or subjective) understanding of such waiver rights is required by the YCJA.

But, having said this, it is another matter to state the level of proof required to show such understanding. That is, how does one prove actual understanding? Here, the Court of Appeal said that the Crown must prove waiver on a balance of probabilities. This is, a lower standard of proof than beyond a reasonable doubt.

THE ROLE OF VIDEOTAPES

Section 146 of the YCJA requires that the statement of a young person be taken either by videotape or in writing. With L.T.H., the statement was taken by videotape.

As we shall see, the videotape allowed the Court to see the demeanour of the constable. By that, we mean the Court could see some of the indicia as to whether the constable intended to communicate with L.T.H. and if he succeeded in that regard.

The videotape allowed the Court to see that the constable apparently intended not to make eye contact with L.T.H. Further, it allowed the Court to see that the constable rushed the waiver questions. (If the waiver were based solely on the written statement, there would be no indication that the waiver questions were rushed.)

The videotape indicated that L.T.H. did not seem take the police interview seriously. This, in turn, allowed the Court to infer that, as a young offender, he was all the more in need of the advice of a lawyer and/or an adult. With more pointed and sensitive police questioning — especially after having been given some warning by L.T.H.'s mother concerning her son's learning difficulties — there might have been greater awareness of how much more was required to ascertain whether there had been any knowing waiver by L.T.H.

THE SUPREME COURT DECIDES

L.T.H. v. The Queen was appealed to the Supreme Court of Canada. A seven-member panel of the Court heard and decided upon the matter. All members of the panel agreed with the result, though three of the justices disagreed with the test that led to that result.

For all the justices, the issue to decide upon was not one of "mere technicality" (see Tibbetts 2008). Justice Fish, who spoke for the Court majority, quoted the statement of principles in the YCJA. He wrote:

> Section 3(b) of the YCJA ... provides that the criminal justice system for young persons must be separate from that of adults and emphasize the following: ... (iii) enhanced procedural protection to ensure that young persons are treated fairly and that their rights, including their right to privacy, are protected.
>
> The procedural rights set out in section 146 represent one instance of the enhanced protection Parliament has seen fit to provide for young persons. The relevant parts of section 146 provide

that no statement by a young person to a person in authority will be admissible in evidence against that young person unless: (1) the statement was voluntary (section 146(2)(a)); (2) the person who took the statement "clearly explained to the young person, in language appropriate to his or her age and understanding," the young person's right to silence and right to consult counsel and another appropriate adult (and the requirement that any person consulted be present during the interview) (section 146(2)(b)); and (3) the young person was given a reasonable opportunity to exercise those rights (section 146(2)(c)).

Finally, section 146(4) provides that young persons, subject to certain conditions, can waive their right to consult counsel and an adult before making the statement and can also waive the right to have counsel and the adult present when the statement is made.

There is purpose to the procedural protections of the YCJA. Justice Fish recited the Court's view of Parliament's reasons for enacting section 146 of the YCJA. He wrote:

This Court has consistently held that the rationale for section 146, and its predecessor (the Young Offenders Act), lies in Parliament's recognition that young persons generally do not understand their legal rights as well as adults, are less likely to assert those rights in the face of a confrontation with a person in authority and are more susceptible to the pressures of interrogation.... Given the purpose of the provision, it would be inconsistent to find that the statutory requirements of section 146 will be complied with whenever a clearly worded form is read to a young person.

Even before the enactment of the YCJA and its predecessor, trial courts recognized that statements made by young persons should be treated differently than statements made by adults. In *The Queen v. Yensen*, [1961] *Ontario Reports* 703 (High Court), for example, McRuer (Chief Judge High Court) held that the interrogating officer must "demonstrate to the Court that the child did understand the caution as a result of careful explanation and pointing out to the child the consequences that may flow from making the statement."

RECOGNIZING REALITY

At the same time, Justice Fish said that the trial court should not turn its head away from reality. He wrote:

The requirement of understanding and appreciation applies to all young persons, including those who are no strangers to the criminal justice system. Section 146(2)(b) incorporates principles of fairness that must be applied uniformly to all without regard to the characteristics of the particular young person.

This does not mean that experience in the criminal justice system is irrelevant to the inquiry as to the young person's understanding. An individualized, objective approach must take into account the level of sophistication of the young detainee and other personal characteristics relevant to the young person's understanding.

Police officers, in determining the appropriate language to use in explaining a young person's rights, must therefore make a reasonable effort to become aware of significant factors of this sort, such as learning disabilities and previous experience with the criminal justice system.

In effect, the police are required to take the individual measure of the young person. Generalities alone will not do.

THE BASIS FOR THE MAJORITY TEST

It was the view of the majority in *L.T.H. v. The Queen* that the test of beyond a reasonable doubt set out in section 146 reflected both the common law and the requirements of section 10 of the Charter. This is how Justice Fish stated the matter:

> Section 146 gives statutory expression to common law rules and constitutional rights that apply to adults and to young persons alike. It provides, for example, that no statement by a young person to a person in authority will be admissible in evidence against that young person unless it is voluntary. And it reaffirms the right to counsel enshrined in section 10 of the Canadian Charter of Rights and Freedoms.
>
> Parliament has recognized in this way that the right to counsel and the right to silence are intimately related. And that relationship is underscored in section 146 by the additional requirements that must be satisfied in order for statements made by young persons to be admissible against them at their trials. Parliament has in this way underscored the generally accepted proposition

that procedural and evidentiary safeguards available to adults do not adequately protect young persons, who are presumed on account of their age and relative unsophistication to be more vulnerable than adults to suggestion, pressure and influence in the hands of police interrogators.

Accordingly, section 146 provides that statements made by young persons are inadmissible against them unless the persons who took them "clearly explained to the young person, in language appropriate to his or her age and understanding," the specific rights conferred by section 146. This condition of admissibility has been referred to as the "informational requirement" of section 146 and it raises two questions that, again, are intimately related.

The first is whether the Crown must prove not only that the necessary explanation was given in appropriate and understandable language, but also that it was in fact understood by the young person who made the statement. The second is whether compliance with the informational requirement must be proved by the Crown beyond a reasonable doubt, or only on a balance of probabilities.

Because of their interdependence ... I would answer both questions together. In my view, the Crown's evidentiary burden will be discharged by clear and convincing evidence that the person to whom the statement was made took reasonable steps to ensure that the young person who made it understood his or her rights under section 146 of the YCJA. A mere probability of compliance is incompatible with the object and scheme of section 146, read as a whole. Compliance must be established beyond a reasonable doubt.

Finally, section 146 provides that young persons, subject to certain conditions, can waive their right under that section to consult with counsel and an adult relative before making a statement and their right to have counsel and the relative present when the statement is made. As we shall see, an unbroken line of authority, beginning with *Korponay v. Attorney General of Canada*, [1982] 1 *Supreme Court of Canada Reports* 41, establishes that a waiver must be established by "clear and unequivocal [evidence] that the person is waiving the procedural safeguard and is doing so with full knowledge of the rights the procedure was enacted to protect and of the effect the waiver will have on those rights in the process." ...

In this case, the trial judge was not satisfied that the Crown discharged its burden under section 146 of the YCJA. She therefore found the appellant's statement inadmissible and ultimately entered an acquittal. The Court of Appeal disagreed. Justice Fish would have allowed the appeal and restored the acquittal at trial.

RECITATION OF RIGHTS: AN APPROPRIATE INDICATION OF UNDERSTANDING?

Police arrested fourteen-year-old R.B. on a charge of car theft. They had carefully reviewed the Court's decision in *L.T.H. v. The Queen*. The police chief and the Crown met and decided that the best way to determine if there had been a proper, lawful waiver was to have the accused, R.B., recite back the waiver provisions in the police waiver form. He did so.

However, such recitation are not fully acceptable within the meaning of section 146 of the YCJA. Justice Fish, in *L.T.H. v. The Queen*, referring to the trial court decision in that case, wrote:

> I take care not to be understood to require police officers, as the trial judge apparently did in this case, to ask young persons in every case to "recite back" or "explain back" their rights.
>
> In some instances, this may well demonstrate that the explanation was both appropriate and sufficient. And it may tend to show that the rights waived were in fact understood — which is of course essential to the validity of the waiver. But "reciting back" or "explaining back" is not transformed by its evident utility into a legal requirement under section 146.

CHALLENGE QUESTION

A ROLE FOR STANDARDIZED FORMS

Q: If police used a standardized form that asked the necessary questions to determine whether an arrested youth intends to waive the right to counsel and/or having an appropriate adult attend police questioning and the taking of any statement, would the youth's answer be useful in determining whether there has been waiver within the meaning of section 146 of the YCJA?

The Court majority in *L.T.H. v. The Queen* clearly held that police should make individualized judgment. This does not rule out the use of standardized forms. Rather, Justice Fish, speaking for the Court majority, said that such forms might be useful as a framework for interrogation. He wrote:

> The reading of a standardized form will not normally suffice in itself to establish the sufficiency of the caution required by section 146(2)(b). Persons in authority must, in addition, acquire some insight into the level of comprehension of the young person concerned, since the mandatory explanation must be appropriate to the age and understanding of that young person. In the words of the Manitoba Court of Appeal in *The Queen v. B.S.M.* (1995), 100 *Manitoba Reports* (2d series) 151:
>
>> The simple reading of an appropriate waiver form to an accused young person will not generally constitute a clear explanation of his rights or of the consequences of signing a waiver. What will constitute a clear explanation will depend on the facts of a particular case. I would suggest that the mere reading of a waiver form accompanied by the repeated question 'Do you understand?' would normally fall short of satisfying the statutory requirements. Parliament has expressly stated that young people

require more than the offering of information. They require not just explanations, but clear explanations that they are able to understand....

Properly crafted and scrupulously applied, standardized forms nonetheless provide a useful framework for the appropriate interrogation of young detainees....

In short, adherence to standardized forms can *facilitate*, but will not always *constitute*, compliance with section 146(2)(b). Compliance is a matter of substance, not form. The trial court must be satisfied, upon considering all of the evidence, that the young person's rights were in fact explained clearly and comprehensibly by the person in authority.

THE CHARTER AND THE YCJA

The Charter is part of the Constitution of Canada. Young people are covered by the rights granted under the Charter. Included in such rights are those related to police questioning. Section 10(b) of the Charter provides, "Everyone has the right on arrest or detention ... to retain and instruct counsel without delay and to be informed of that right...."

The Charter sets the minimum requirements relating to the right to counsel. There is nothing in the Charter that prohibits Parliament from enlarging the rights afforded. And that is just what Parliament has done through section 146 of the YCJA.

What role, then, does the Charter play in interpreting and applying section 146 of the YCJA? The answer, in part, comes through the opinion of Justice Fish, speaking for the Court majority in *L.T.H. v. The Queen*.

Section 146 is not to be given a narrow reading. It is not to be construed as any other law. Rather, it is to be interpreted in a broad "purposive" way to achieve the legislative goal designed to protect those deemed "vulnerable" — the young.

DIFFERENCES

So it is that the Court majority differed from the partial dissent of Justice Rothstein (concurred in by Justices Deschamps and Charron). Justice Rothstein would have applied common law rules of interpretation that would have placed a lesser burden on the trial judge in making findings of fact. The test he would have used to determine the acceptability of such trial court findings would have been the preponderance of the evidence.

Justice Rothstein wrote:

> I have read the reasons of Justice Fish. He says that the Crown's evidentiary burden will be discharged by evidence that the person to whom the statement was made has, before the statement is made, clearly explained to the young person, in language appropriate to his or her age and understanding, his or her rights under section 146(2)(b) of the YCJA. Evidence of actual understanding is not required. I agree. I also agree with him that the young person's previous experience in the youth criminal justice system may be evidence that the caution was explained in language appropriate to the young person's understanding.

As to the second issue, I agree with Fish J. that the Crown must prove beyond a reasonable doubt that the statement made by the young person was voluntary. I differ with him, however, on the standard of proof applicable to whether there was compliance by the person in authority with the informational and waiver requirements of section 146 of the YCJA. Fish J. says the standard is proof beyond a reasonable doubt. In my respectful view, the standard is proof on a balance of probabilities....

I do agree that Parliament specifically sought to endow young persons with enhanced procedural protections in the form of the statutorily based protections in section 146 in recognition of the presumption of reduced moral sophistication and maturity of young persons. Parliament did not say, however, that the standard of proof for compliance with the informational and waiver requirements is beyond a reasonable doubt. To the contrary, Parliament stated in section 146(1) of the YCJA that the common law rule relating to the admissibility of evidence is to apply — namely, that all preliminary findings of fact relating to the use of evidence, other than voluntariness, must be determined on the balance of probabilities.

The requirements of section 146 are substantially broader than those under the Canadian Charter of Rights and Freedoms. A young person must be advised of the right to silence and warned of the potential use of any statement against him or her, as well as of the right to consult with counsel and a parent and to have those persons present while a statement is made (section 146(2)(b) of the YCJA). If any of these requirements are not satisfied, the statement will automatically be inadmissible (section 146(2) of the YCJA). In contrast, an adult only has to be informed of the reason for arrest and the right to retain counsel (section 10(a) and (b) of the Charter). Police may question an adult who has retained counsel in the absence of that legal adviser, unless the accused asks for counsel to be present. "Police persuasion, short of denying the suspect the right to choose or depriving him of an operating mind, does not breach the right to silence" (*The Queen v. Hebert*, [1990] 2 *Supreme Court of Canada Reports* 151, at p. 184, and quoted with approval in *Singh*, at para. 46). In the case of young persons, however, any statement made by the young person is required to be made in the presence of counsel and any other person requested by the young person, unless the young person desires otherwise (section 146(2)(b)(iv) of the YCJA).

It is by affording young persons the additional protections expressed in section 146 of the YCJA that Parliament satisfied its objective of recognizing the reduced sophistication and maturity of young persons. There is nothing in the words of section 146 that expresses or implies a standard of proof of beyond a reasonable doubt for preliminary determinations of fact. To the contrary, section 146 explicitly incorporates the applicable common law standard of proof with respect to the admissibility of evidence, namely, proof on a balance of probabilities for preliminary findings of fact.

The Court majority, however, imposed a more rigid test: The findings of the trial judge must be sustained beyond a reasonable doubt. This conclusion, said Justice Fish, better allowed the purpose of the YCJA to be carried forward. And that purpose overrode whatever might have been the common law rules of interpretation.

YOU BE THE JUDGE

LOOKING LIKE A SUSPECT

THE FACTS

Janet Soames, a police officer for the town of Britby, was a veteran with fifteen years of service. Much of that time had been spent patrolling downtown public housing developments where, as it happened, youth gangs were prevalent. For several weeks, she had watched one person in particular. He was a newcomer to the area who went by the name of Jamie Y. He was tall and muscular, and appeared to be about eighteen years old.

She was interested in him because he seemed to regularly associate with much younger youths, who appeared to be about twelve to fourteen years old. Further, Jamie not only had taken a leadership role in what the constable saw as an emerging gang, but the "games" played seem inordinately aggressive.

Constable Soames introduced herself to Jamie, and she had a number of conversations with him. She described his attitude toward her as "polite, but with a sneering undertone." She asked him his age, and he responded, "I am old enough to know that I don't have to give you that information." With that, he walked away, while his friends, Constable Soames said, "looked on admiringly."

Not long after that incident, a local variety store reported that the purse of an elderly customer who was leaving the store had been snatched by a young person, tall, and about eighteen years old. The description generally seemed to match that of Jamie.

The day after receiving the report, Constable Soames arrested Jamie on suspicion that he was the one who had grabbed the elderly woman's purse. At the police station, she again asked Jamie his age. He angrily said, "Treat me like an adult. I don't need a lawyer, or anyone else. I know how to deal with cops."

Constable Soames said that she didn't want to "take any chances" concerning whether Jamie was covered by the YCJA. Moreover, both she and her chief wanted to "get this case resolved quickly." There was some fear of a possible rash of petty robberies from newly formed youth gangs.

For reasons unknown to the police, Jamie's school had misplaced records of his home address and the identities of his parents. Still, Constable Soames, on the off-chance that Jamie might be a youth covered by the YCJA, gave him the opportunity to have a lawyer and/or his parents (or any other adult) present during his interrogation and any statement resulting from such questioning. Jamie, refusing to give his age, clearly and angrily refused the offer.

Jamie was questioned aggressively but fairly. He admitted that he was "on the watch" for "possible suckers, easy prey." But he denied that he had snatched the purse of the elderly victim. "I don't pick on old people," he said.

A statement reflecting Jamie's responses to police questioning was completed. Jamie read and signed it, along with a waiver stating that he did not want a lawyer or an adult present during the police questioning.

Later, Jamie was presented in a line-up for identification. The victim identified him as the person who had snatched her purse. Jamie was charged, and only at his preliminary hearing did it become known that he was fifteen years old.

At that point, Jamie claimed, through court-appointed counsel, that the waiver he gave police was not valid and, therefore, all that followed from the identification to the preliminary hearing was invalid.

THE ISSUE

Did the Crown have to give Jamie any further opportunity for a lawyer and/or adult to have been present at the time of his detention?

POINTS TO CONSIDER

- Section 10(b) of the Charter provides that "Everyone has the right on arrest or detention to retain and instruct counsel without delay and to be informed of that right."
- Section 146 of the YCJA gives an arrested or detained youth the right to waive the right to a lawyer or adult representation.
- No intimidation nor threats were used by police in questioning Jamie.
- Section 146(2) of the YCJA provides, "No oral or written statement made by a young person who is less than eighteen years old, to a peace

officer or to any other person who is, in law, a person in authority, on the arrest or detention of the young person or in circumstances where the peace officer or other person has reasonable grounds for believing that the young person has committed an offence is admissible against the young person unless the statement was voluntary."

DISCUSSION

There is a strong possibility that the statement, itself, will be rejected by the court. The reason: section 146 goes on to put some rather specific content into what constitutes a "voluntary" statement — one that amounts to a waiver of the right to lawyer, and/or the right to have a parent or another appropriate adult present during any questioning and/or taking of any statement. And it is questionable whether Constable Soames met those conditions.

1. It is true that section 146 does allow a young person covered by its terms to waive the right to counsel and/or the presence of an adult in any police questioning. However, section 146(b)(ii) requires the police before taking a statement to inform the young person that he is under no obligation to make a statement. Constable Soames did not inform Jamie that he did not have to make a statement.

2. It is also true that that Constable Soames made an effort to find Jamie's parents. Section 146(8)(b) allows the trial judge to accept any statement made by a young person if the police officer (or "other person in authority")

made reasonable inquiries as to the young person's age and had reasonable grounds for believing that person was eighteen years old or older.

Here, in part, the question is whether reasonable efforts were made to determine Jamie's age. In the final analysis, that is a question of fact for the judge to determine. Remember that Constable Soames was not sure of Jamie's age. When she first encountered him, he was associating with young teenagers who appeared to be twelve to fourteen years old.

In any event, even if Constable Soames had reason to believe that Jamie was eighteen, there remained the failure of the police to inform Jamie that he didn't have to make any statement. This right to be silent, while it is included in YCJA, also emanates from the Charter of Rights and Freedoms. (More will be said of this right in the "You Be the Judge: The Case of the 'Trick.'")

THE SPONTANEOUS STATEMENT

Let's change the facts somewhat. Suppose that at the time Constable Soames arrested Jamie, he had said, "I know why you're arresting me. It's about that old lady's bag. Well, guess what? I did it! So, what are you going to do about it?"

Constable Soames did not have time to caution Jamie. She didn't have time to tell Jamie that he had a right to counsel or a parent or an adult's advice. He had the right to remain silent.

Section 146 of the YCJA would not prohibit Constable Soames from testifying at Jamie's trial as to what was said at the time of arrest. Section 146(3) of the YCJA relates to oral statements. It provides:

"The requirements set out in paragraphs (2)(b) to (d) do not apply in respect of oral statements if they are made spontaneously by the young person to a peace officer or other person in authority before that person has had a reasonable opportunity to comply with those requirements." Bear in mind, however, that it is the Crown that carries the burden of proof in demonstrating that Constable Soames did not have reasonable time to tell Jamie of his right to a lawyer and/or an adult to advise him.

YOU BE THE JUDGE

THE CASE OF THE "TRICK"

Here our concern is not so much with the YCJA as with the Charter.

THE FACTS

Sally, age seventeen, was arrested and charged with theft. The police were aware that she was a young person within the meaning of the YCJA. They afforded her the right to counsel and to reach her parents and/or an appropriate adult and to consult with them before any questioning or before any statement was taken. Further, Sally was told that she did not have to give a statement.

Sally, through her parents, reached and spoke with a lawyer; she also spoke with her parents and another adult (a close friend of the family). The police then asked her if she was ready to make a statement. Her answer was a clear and strong "no." She didn't want to make any statement to the police. She said, "I'll take my chances in court."

Investigating police officers believed, however, not only that Sally had committed the alleged theft, but that she also was deeply involved in a youth gang. With their superior's approval, they put Sally in a detention room with an officer in disguise as a suspect. The officer looked like a teenager.

The officer's assignment was to get Sally to talk. She was successful. Sally made a number of highly incriminating statements not only about the alleged theft, but also about her activities with a youth gang.

At Sally's trial on the charge of theft, the formerly disguised officer was called to testify. Her evidence was central to the Crown's prosecution. Sally's lawyer moved to strike such testimony and, because it was so incriminating, to have the charge against Sally dismissed.

THE ISSUE

Are Sally's statements to the undercover police officer protected?

POINTS TO CONSIDER

- The undercover police officer acted on instructions from her superior.
- The YCJA provisions relating to the right to counsel and advice of an adult, including parents, were satisfied. The undercover agent took no statement from Sally. Rather, she listened and reported what Sally said.
- Section 7 of the Charter provides, "Everyone has the right to life, liberty and security of the

person and the right not to be deprived thereof except in accordance with the principles of fundamental justice."

- Section 10 of the Charter provides, "Everyone has the right on arrest or detention ... (b) to retain and instruct counsel without delay and to be informed of that right."

- Section 24(2) of the Charter provides, "Where in proceedings [such as those before a youth court involving the charge of theft] a court concludes that evidence was obtained in a manner that infringed or denied any rights or freedoms guaranteed by this Charter, the evidence shall be excluded if it is established that, having regard to all the circumstances, the admission of it in the proceedings would bring the administration of justice into disrepute."

DISCUSSION

The testimony of the undercover agent likely will be rejected by the court. And, since that testimony is central to the prosecution, the charge against Sally probably would be dismissed.

It is true that the YCJA provides in section 146(2)(b)(i) the following: "the person to whom the statement was made has, before the statement was made, clearly explained to the young person, in language appropriate to his or her age and understanding, that the young person is under no obligation to make a statement."

Here, however, we are not dealing with a statement, as such, but rather with a conversation with an undercover agent. Further, the rights being asserted by Sally are those under the Charter, not statute.

The start-point in the discussion of this case is not the YCJA. In a broad sense, on the facts as given, the terms of that law have been satisfied, at least insofar as the right to consult with a lawyer, parents, and/or an adult. Sally refused to give a statement to the police, and they did not press her on that matter.

For the Court, the question is rather whether the Charter affords a constitutional right to be silent.

The Charter and the rights granted under it apply to everyone — including young persons.

THE RIGHT TO BE SILENT

The exercise in "You Be the Judge: The Case of the 'Trick'" was built on the case of *The Queen v. Hebert* [1990] 2 *Supreme Court of Canada Reports* 151. While the facts in this case related to an adult male, the same reasoning would apply to a young person. The Court denied the Crown the use of the statements made to the undercover agent. It upheld the right of the detained person to remain silent.

Then Justice McLachlin (now chief justice) spoke for the Court majority. She stated:

> The Charter, through section 7, seeks to impose limits on the power of the state over the detained person. It thus seeks to effect a balance between the interests of the detained individual and those of the state. On the one hand, section 7 seeks to provide to a person involved in the judicial process protection against unfair use

by the state of its superior resources. On the other hand, it maintains to the state the power to deprive a person of life, liberty or security of the person provided it respects fundamental principles of justice.

The balance is critical. Too much emphasis on either of these purposes may bring the administration of justice into disrepute — in the first case because the state has used its superior power against the individual, in the second because the state's legitimate interest in law enforcement has been frustrated without proper justification.

The right to silence conferred by section 7 reflects these values. The suspect, although placed in the superior power of the state upon detention, retains the right to choose whether or not he will make a statement to the police. To this end, the Charter requires that the suspect be informed of his or her right to counsel without delay. If the suspect chooses to make a statement, the suspect may do so. But, if the suspect chooses not to, the state is not entitled to use its superior power to override the suspect's will and negate his or her choice.

The scope of the right to silence must be defined broadly enough to preserve for the detained person the right to choose whether to speak to the authorities or to remain silent, notwithstanding the fact that he or she is in the superior power of the state. On this view, the scope of the [Charter] right must extend to exclude tricks that would effectively deprive the suspect of his choice. To permit the authorities to trick the suspect into making a confession to them after he or she has exercised the right of conferring with counsel and declined to make a statement, is to permit the authorities to do indirectly what the Charter does not permit them to do directly. This cannot be in accordance with the purpose of the Charter.

Charter provisions related to the right to silence of a detained person under section 7 suggest that the right must be interpreted in a manner which secures to the detained person the right to make a free and meaningful choice as to whether to speak with authorities or to remain silent. A lesser protection would be inconsistent not only with the implications of the right to counsel and the right against self-incrimination affirmed by the Charter, but with the underlying philosophy and purpose of the procedural guarantees the Charter enshrines.

THE REMEDY

What remedy should the Court impose for the Crown's violation of the accused's right to be silent? (Bear in mind, if there were a violation of the YCJA as to the improper taking of a young person's statement by a person in authority — such as the police — the Act clearly allows the youth court judge to refuse its use in the criminal proceeding.)

Section 24(2) of the Charter allows a court to deny the use of the police officer's testimony where there has been a violation of the Charter right to silence and where receiving such evidence would bring the administration of justice into disrepute. Justice McLachlin, again speaking for the Court majority, ruled that it would be highly prejudicial to the accused to allow the police officer's narration of what was said to be used in evidence. She stated:

> I am of the view that the evidence sought to be adduced in this case would render the trial unfair. I should not be taken as suggesting that violation of the accused's right to silence under section 7 automatically means that the evidence must be excluded under section 24(2). I would not wish to rule out the possibility that there may be circumstances in which a statement might be received where the suspect has not been accorded a full choice in the sense of having decided, after full observance of all rights, to make a statement voluntarily.
>
> But where, as here, an accused is conscripted to give evidence against himself after clearly electing not to do so by use of an *unfair trick* [emphasis added] practised by the authorities, and where the resultant statement is the only evidence against him, one must surely conclude that reception of such evidence would render the trial unfair. The accused would be deprived of his/her presumption of innocence and

would be placed in a position of having to take the stand if he/she wished to counter the damaging effect of the confession. The accused's conviction if obtained would rest almost entirely on his own evidence against himself, obtained by a trick in violation of the Charter.

I am also satisfied that the Charter violation was a serious one. The conduct of the police was willful and deliberate. They intentionally set out on a course to undermine the [accused's] right to silence notwithstanding his expressed assertion of that right, by having the undercover police officer engage him in conversation. It is said the police acted in good faith.... However, ignorance of the effect of the Charter does not preclude application of section 24(2) of the Charter....

The effect of the exclusion [of the undercover officer's testimony] in this case is serious. It would result in an acquittal, since virtually the only evidence was his statement to the undercover policeman.

Balancing these factors, I arrive at the conclusion that the test of section 24(2) is met. As the [case] authorities ... amply demonstrate, it has long been felt inappropriate that an accused should be required to betray himself. Where virtually the only evidence against him is such betrayal, the effect is that the accused is required to secure his own conviction. That is contrary to the notions of justice fundamental to our system of law and calculated, in my opinion, to bring the administration of justice into disrepute.

CHALLENGE QUESTION

THE JAILHOUSE STOOL PIGEON

Q: Will the court receive the evidence of the "jailhouse" informant over a defendant's objection as to her Charter right to remain silent?

Suppose we have the same facts as in "You Be the Judge: The Case of the 'Trick,'" but with this difference: The police place the accused in a detention room with another person charged with a serious offence. That person has a long criminal record, and she thinks there is a way to get the Crown to "go easy" on her. Unknown to the police and the Crown, she gets information from Sally — enough information so that if her testimony were accepted, there is little doubt that Sally would be convicted. In the parlance of the criminal world, this person is known as a "jailhouse stool pigeon."

The court in all likelihood would receive such evidence. Justice Sopinka, concurring in the Hebert case (*The Queen v. Hebert* [1990] 2 *Supreme Court of Canada Reports* 151) said, in effect, that such an informant would not be a person "in authority." She was not solicited to gather such information for the Crown or the police.

Justice Sopinka wrote:

> So, for example, the use of a wire on a police informant in a conversation between the informant and an uncharged suspect, as described in *The Queen v. Thatcher*, [1987] 1 *Supreme Court of Canada Reports* 652, at pp. 668–69, would not implicate the constitutional right to remain silent.
>
> Furthermore, even after charge and during detention, the right to remain silent would not be violated by the passive surveillance of a conversation between an accused and another (genuine) prisoner by an undercover officer, or an electronic device: see *The Queen v. Smith, Wilson and Quesnelle,* Ontario Supreme Court, November 5, 1987, unreported, in which Reid J. drew this distinction. (Though, it should be noted that in cases of electronic "participant surveillance," different constitutional issues arise pursuant to section 8 of the Charter: see *The Queen v. Duarte,* [1990] 1 *Supreme Court of Canada Reports* 30.)

Her testimony, however, would be given limited weight largely because (1) while she was not promised a lighter sentence on conviction, she acted, in part, on the hope that her sentence would be lessened and (2) her past convictions, especially if they involved matters of credibility, such as fraud, would be brought out in cross-examination.

REFERENCES AND FURTHER READING

Hoffman, Jan. 1998a. "Police Are Skirting Restraints to Get Confessions." *New York Times*, March 29.

_____. 1998b. "Police Refine Methods So Potent Even the Innocent Have Confessed." *New York Times*, March 30.

"Interrogators Must Tailor Questioning of Youth, Top Court Rules." 2008. *CBC.ca*, September 11.

Makin, Kirk. 2008. "N.S. Teen With Disability Did Not Understand Rights, Court Rules." *Globe and Mail*, September 12.

Tibbetts, Janice. 2008. "Supreme Court Acquits Nova Scotia Teen on a Charter Technicality." *National Post*, September 11.

APPENDIX

YOUTH CRIMINAL JUSTICE ACT: SECTION 146

(1) Subject to this section, the law relating to the admissibility of statements made by persons accused of committing offences applies in respect of young persons.

(2) No oral or written statement made by a young person who is less than eighteen years old, to a peace officer or to any other person who is, in law, a person in authority, on the arrest or detention of the young person or in circumstances where the peace officer or other person has reasonable grounds for believing that the young person has committed an offence is admissible against the young person unless

> (a) the statement was voluntary;

> (b) the person to whom the statement was made has, before the statement was made, clearly explained to the young person, in language appropriate to his or her age and understanding, that

>> (i) the young person is under no obligation to make a statement,

(ii) any statement made by the young person may be used as evidence in proceedings against him or her,

(iii) the young person has the right to consult counsel and a parent or other person in accordance with paragraph (c), and

(iv) any statement made by the young person is required to be made in the presence of counsel and any other person consulted in accordance with paragraph (c), if any, unless the young person desires otherwise;

(c) the young person has, before the statement was made, been given a reasonable opportunity to consult

(i) with counsel, and

(ii) with a parent or, in the absence of a parent, an adult relative or, in the absence of a parent and an adult relative, any other appropriate adult chosen by the young person, as long as that person is not a co-accused, or under investigation, in respect of the same offence; and

(d) if the young person consults a person in accordance with paragraph (c), the young person has been given a reasonable opportunity to make the statement in the presence of that person.

(3) The requirements set out in paragraphs (2)(b) to (d) do not apply in respect of oral statements if they are made spontaneously by the young person to a peace officer or other person in authority before that person has had a reasonable opportunity to comply with those requirements.

(4) A young person may waive the rights under paragraph (2)(c) or (d) but any such waiver

    (a) must be recorded on video tape or audio tape; or

    (b) must be in writing and contain a statement signed by the young person that he or she has been informed of the right being waived.

(5) When a waiver of rights under paragraph (2)(c) or (d) is not made in accordance with subsection (4) owing to a technical irregularity, the youth justice court may determine that the waiver is valid if it is satisfied that the young person was informed of his or her rights, and voluntarily waived them.

(6) When there has been a technical irregularity in complying with paragraphs (2)(b) to (d), the youth justice court may admit into evidence a statement referred to in subsection (2), if satisfied that the admission of the statement would not bring into disrepute the principle that young persons are entitled to enhanced procedural protection to ensure that they are treated fairly and their rights are protected.

(7) A youth justice court judge may rule inadmissible in any proceedings under this Act a statement made by the young person in respect of whom the proceedings are taken if the young person

satisfies the judge that the statement was made under duress imposed by any person who is not, in law, a person in authority.

(8) A youth justice court judge may in any proceedings under this Act rule admissible any statement or waiver by a young person if, at the time of the making of the statement or waiver,

> (a) the young person held himself or herself to be eighteen years old or older;

> (b) the person to whom the statement or waiver was made conducted reasonable inquiries as to the age of the young person and had reasonable grounds for believing that the young person was eighteen years old or older; and

> (c) in all other circumstances the statement or waiver would otherwise be admissible.

(9) For the purpose of this section, a person consulted under paragraph (2)(c) is, in the absence of evidence to the contrary, deemed not to be a person in authority.

INDEX

COMING JULY 2014
UNDERSTANDING CANADIAN LAW
SERIES:

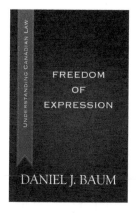

Freedom of Expression
By Daniel J. Baum
$14.99
9781459723177

Freedom of expression is a fundamental right protected by the Charter of Rights and Freedoms, which is part of the Constitution of Canada. But even that right has limits. Peacefully picketing an abortion clinic, so long as patients can come and go, is a protected right, but shouting "Fire!" in a crowded theatre to cause a stampede is a criminal offence. This book explains how our courts interpret the term "freedom of speech" and explains the difference between expressing one's views freely and infringing upon the rights of others.

ALSO FROM DUNDURN:

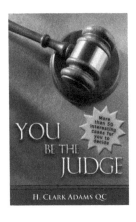

You Be the Judge
By H. Clark Adams
$19.99
9781554889785

It's enough to put you off wedded bliss forever, but if you did harbour strong opinions on how the case Smith v. Brown — a couple on the brink of matrimony, interfering relatives notwithstanding — should unfold, H. Clark Adams welcomes you to the legal arena of small claims court. Here feuding former lovers, despondent homeowners, and singed shopkeepers bring their grievances against their erstwhile partners in love and business for a ruling that could end the troubled relationship and maybe even offer them material or monetary comfort.

In a tone that's distinctly light-hearted, the retired deputy judge offers readers a fictionalized sampling of the cases presented at small claims court, and the chance for them to pit their best instincts and powers of judgment against his. Part 1 of the book is a collection of cases from the gripping to the ridiculous, while, Part 2 features Adams's decisions on the cases presented. If your view on these sixty cases differs from the learned judge, be warned: no appeal to his decision has ever been successful.

The Canadian Constitution
By Adam Dodek
$12.99
9781459709317

The Canadian Constitution makes Canada's Constitution readily accessible to readers for the first time. It includes the complete text of the Constitution Acts of 1867 and 1982 as well as a glossary of key terms, a short history of the Constitution, and a timeline of important constitutional events. *The Canadian Constitution* also explains how the Supreme Court of Canada works and describes the people and issues involved in leading constitutional cases.

Author Adam Dodek, a law professor at the University of Ottawa, provides the only index to the Canadian Constitution as well as fascinating facts about the Supreme Court and the Constitution that have never been published before. This book is a great primer for those coming to Canada's Constitution for the first time as well as a useful reference work for students and scholars.

Available at your favourite bookseller

VISIT US AT
Dundurn.com
@dundurnpress
Facebook.com/dundurnpress
Pinterest.com/dundurnpress